TEACHER'S PET PUBLICATIONS

PUZZLE PACK
for
To Kill a Mockingbird

based on the book by
Harper Lee

Written by
William T. Collins

© 2005 Teacher's Pet Publications
All Rights Reserved

The materials in this packet are copyrighted
by Teacher's Pet Publications, Inc.

These pages may be duplicated by the purchaser
for use in the purchaser's own classroom.

Copying any of these materials and distributing them
for any other purpose is a violation of the copyright laws.

© 2005 Teacher's Pet Publications, Inc.
www.tpet.com

INTRODUCTION
If you already own the LitPlan for this title, this Puzzle Pack will refresh your Unit Resource Materials and Vocabulary Resource Materials sections plus give you additional materials you can substitute into the tests. If you do not already have a complete LitPlan, these pages will give you some supplemental materials to use with your own plan. There are two main groups of materials: one set for unit words (such as characters' names, symbols, places, etc.) and one set for vocabulary words associated with the book.

WORD LIST
There is a word list for both the unit words and the vocabulary words. These lists show you which words are being used in the materials and the clues or definitions being used for those words. You may want to give students a word list with clues/definitions to help them, or you may want students to only have a word list (without clues/definitions) if you want them to work a little harder. Both are available for duplication. The word lists can also be your "calling key" for the bingo games.

FILL IN THE BLANK AND MATCHING
There are 4 each of the fill in the blank and matching worksheets for both the unit and vocabulary words. These pages can be used either as extra worksheets for students or as objective parts of a unit test. They can be done individually if students need extra help or as a whole class activity to review the material covered.

MAGIC SQUARES
The magic squares not only reinforce the material covered but also work on reasoning and math skills. Many teachers have told us that their students really enjoy doing these!

WORD SEARCH PUZZLES
The word search words go in all directions, as indicated on your answer keys. Two of the word search puzzles have the clues listed rather than the words. This makes the puzzle a little more difficult, but it reinforces the material better. Two word search puzzles have words only for students who find the clue puzzles too difficult.

CROSSWORD PUZZLES
Both unit and vocabulary word sections have 4 crossword puzzles.

BINGO CARDS
There are 32 individual bingo cards for the unit words and 32 individual bingo cards for the vocabulary words. You can use your word list as a "call list," calling the words at random and marking them off of your list as you go, or you could use the flash cards by cutting them apart and drawing the words at random from a hat (or box or whatever). To make a better review, you might ask for the definition and spelling of each word as you call it out–or you could call out the definitions and have students tell you the words they need to look for on the puzzle.

JUGGLE LETTERS
The vocabulary juggle letter game is intended to help students learn the spellings of the words. One sheet has the definitions listed on it as an extra help for students who need it or to reinforce the definitions if you choose to do so.

FLASH CARDS
We've included a set of vocabulary flash cards you can duplicate, cut, and fold for your students. Some teachers make a few sets for general use by the class; others make a set for each student. Some teachers duplicate them for each student and have the students cut & fold their own. You can cut out just the words and put them in a hat, have each student pick out one word and write the definition and a sentence for that word. Students then swap words and papers, with the next student adding a sentence of his own under the last one. You can have students swap as many times as you like. Each time the student will read the sentences written prior to his own and then add a sentence. You can cut out the words and definitions separately and play "I Have; Who Has?" Each student in the room draws a word and definition. The first student says, "I have (the name of the word). Who has the definition?" The student with the definition reads it then says, "I have (the name of the vocabulary word she has). Who has the definition?" The round continues until all words and definitions have been given.

To Kill A Mockingbird Word List

No.	Word	Clue/Definition
1.	ALEXANDRA	Atticus's sister
2.	ARM	Tom's left one had been cut off
3.	ATTICUS	Mr. Finch; Scout's dad
4.	AUTHOR	Harper Lee
5.	AZALEAS	Miss Maudie's flowers
6.	BACKGROUND	The Cunninghams didn't have the proper --- to suit Alexandra
7.	BALCONY	Place from which Scout watched the trial
8.	BOO	Object of the Radley Games
9.	BRAVERY	Courage
10.	BRUISES	Mayella's right side had lots of these
11.	CAKES	Miss Maudie made little ones for the children
12.	CALPURNIA	Finch housekeeper, cook & nanny
13.	CAROLINE	Miss Fisher
14.	CBH	Dill's initials
15.	CECIL	The Jacobs boy
16.	CEMENT	It plugged up the tree hole
17.	CHURCH	Scout and Jem went to Calpurnia's
18.	COMPANY	'He ain't ---, Cal, he's a Cunningham.'
19.	COOTIES	What Burris Ewell had to go home and wash out
20.	COURTROOM	Where trials take place
21.	CRAWFORD	Gossipy neighbor
22.	CRIED	What Jem did after he heard the verdict
23.	CUNNINGHAM	Walter
24.	DILL	Charles Baker Harris
25.	DIRT	Cal rubbed Walter's nose in it
26.	DOG	Atticus shot a mad one
27.	DUBOSE	Jem chopped the tops off her camellia bushes
28.	EDUCATION	What one gets at school
29.	ESCAPE	Tom was shot while trying to ----
30.	EVIDENCE	Material proof
31.	EWELL	Bob or Mayella
32.	FIGURES	Two of these carved from soap were in the tree
33.	FINCH	Scout, Jem or Atticus, for example
34.	FIRE	It destroyed Miss Maudie's home
35.	GAME	The kids played the Boo Radley ----
36.	GILMER	The prosecutor
37.	GUILTY	The jury's verdict
38.	GUM	Object found in the tree
39.	HAM	Scout's pageant costume
40.	HELEN	Mrs. Robinson
41.	HYPOCRITE	Word to describe Miss Gates
42.	INSIDE	Where Boo spent most of his time
43.	JACK	Atticus's brother
44.	JAIL	It housed Tom Robinson while he waited for a trial
45.	JEM	Scout's brother
46.	JURY	12 who decide
47.	KIDS	Scout, Jem and Dill, for example; children
48.	KILL	To end the life of something
49.	KNIFE	Instrument that killed Bob Ewell
50.	LAWYER	Atticus's occupation
51.	LEE	Harper; author

To Kill A Mockingbird Word List Continued

No.	Word	Clue/Definition
52.	LINK	Mr. Deas; He escorted Helen
53.	LULA	Woman at Cal's church who made Scout feel unwelcome
54.	MAUDIE	Neighbor who liked the children & made cakes
55.	MAYCOMB	Name of the town and county
56.	MAYELLA	She was allegedly raped
57.	MISSIONARY	Mrs. Merriweather's ---- circle
58.	MOB	They wanted to inflict their own justice on Tom
59.	MOCKINGBIRD	To Kill A -----
60.	NORMAL	What Scout wanted Boo to be
61.	PAGEANT	Scout made a late entry and ruined it
62.	PANTS	Jem's got caught on the fence
63.	PENNIES	Indian head ones were in the tree
64.	PREJUDICE	Preconceived idea
65.	PRIDE	Mr. Cunningham had this; he would not take charity
66.	PULITZER	Harper Lee won the --- Prize for Mockingbird
67.	RAYMOND	Dolphus
68.	READ	Jem had to do it for Mrs. Dubose
69.	ROBINSON	Tom
70.	SCHOOL	Miss Fisher's work place
71.	SCOUT	Narrator
72.	SHOT	Tom was --- trying to escape
73.	SUMMER	Time of year when Dill visited usually
74.	SYKES	Rev. at Cal's church
75.	TATE	Heck; the sheriff
76.	TAYLOR	The judge for Tom's trial
77.	TO	-- Kill A Mockingbird
78.	TREE	The hiding place for trinkets
79.	TRIAL	Process by which innocence or guilt is determined
80.	WALTER	Boy Cunningham
81.	YARD	Jem pushed Scout into the Radley's ---
82.	ZEEBO	Cal's boy
83.	TRIAL	Process by which innocence or guilt is determined
84.	WALTER	Boy Cunningham
85.	YARD	Jem pushed Scout into the Radley's ---
86.	ZEEBO	Cal's boy

Copyrighted

To Kill A Mockingbird Fill In The Blank 1

_____ 1. Cal's boy

_____ 2. It housed Tom Robinson while he waited for a trial

_____ 3. Mr. Deas; He escorted Helen

_____ 4. Cal rubbed Walter's nose in it

_____ 5. To Kill A -----

_____ 6. Jem pushed Scout into the Radley's ---

_____ 7. Heck; the sheriff

_____ 8. Mayella's right side had lots of these

_____ 9. Miss Fisher's work place

_____ 10. Indian head ones were in the tree

_____ 11. Mr. Cunningham had this; he would not take charity

_____ 12. What one gets at school

_____ 13. Scout, Jem or Atticus, for example

_____ 14. The judge for Tom's trial

_____ 15. Time of year when Dill visited usually

_____ 16. The jury's verdict

_____ 17. Scout's pageant costume

_____ 18. It plugged up the tree hole

_____ 19. Tom

_____ 20. She was allegedly raped

To Kill A Mockingbird Fill In The Blank 1 Answer Key

ZEEBO	1. Cal's boy
JAIL	2. It housed Tom Robinson while he waited for a trial
LINK	3. Mr. Deas; He escorted Helen
DIRT	4. Cal rubbed Walter's nose in it
MOCKINGBIRD	5. To Kill A -----
YARD	6. Jem pushed Scout into the Radley's ---
TATE	7. Heck; the sheriff
BRUISES	8. Mayella's right side had lots of these
SCHOOL	9. Miss Fisher's work place
PENNIES	10. Indian head ones were in the tree
PRIDE	11. Mr. Cunningham had this; he would not take charity
EDUCATION	12. What one gets at school
FINCH	13. Scout, Jem or Atticus, for example
TAYLOR	14. The judge for Tom's trial
SUMMER	15. Time of year when Dill visited usually
GUILTY	16. The jury's verdict
HAM	17. Scout's pageant costume
CEMENT	18. It plugged up the tree hole
ROBINSON	19. Tom
MAYELLA	20. She was allegedly raped

To Kill A Mockingbird Fill In The Blank 2

_____ 1. Finch housekeeper, cook & nanny

_____ 2. Time of year when Dill visited usually

_____ 3. To Kill A -----

_____ 4. Harper; author

_____ 5. Boy Cunningham

_____ 6. It plugged up the tree hole

_____ 7. Scout's pageant costume

_____ 8. It housed Tom Robinson while he waited for a trial

_____ 9. Tom was shot while trying to ----

_____ 10. Heck; the sheriff

_____ 11. The Cunninghams didn't have the proper --- to suit Alexandra

_____ 12. Narrator

_____ 13. Tom's left one had been cut off

_____ 14. Woman at Cal's church who made Scout feel unwelcome

_____ 15. Object of the Radley Games

_____ 16. Mrs. Merriweather's ---- circle

_____ 17. Where trials take place

_____ 18. -- Kill A Mockingbird

_____ 19. Harper Lee

_____ 20. Atticus's occupation

To Kill A Mockingbird Fill In The Blank 2 Answer Key

CALPURNIA	1. Finch housekeeper, cook & nanny
SUMMER	2. Time of year when Dill visited usually
MOCKINGBIRD	3. To Kill A -----
LEE	4. Harper; author
WALTER	5. Boy Cunningham
CEMENT	6. It plugged up the tree hole
HAM	7. Scout's pageant costume
JAIL	8. It housed Tom Robinson while he waited for a trial
ESCAPE	9. Tom was shot while trying to ----
TATE	10. Heck; the sheriff
BACKGROUND	11. The Cunninghams didn't have the proper --- to suit Alexandra
SCOUT	12. Narrator
ARM	13. Tom's left one had been cut off
LULA	14. Woman at Cal's church who made Scout feel unwelcome
BOO	15. Object of the Radley Games
MISSIONARY	16. Mrs. Merriweather's ---- circle
COURTROOM	17. Where trials take place
TO	18. -- Kill A Mockingbird
AUTHOR	19. Harper Lee
LAWYER	20. Atticus's occupation

To Kill A Mockingbird Fill In The Blank 3

_____ 1. Atticus's brother

_____ 2. Where trials take place

_____ 3. Boy Cunningham

_____ 4. Neighbor who liked the children & made cakes

_____ 5. Jem had to do it for Mrs. Dubose

_____ 6. Tom's left one had been cut off

_____ 7. Harper Lee

_____ 8. Atticus's sister

_____ 9. To end the life of something

_____ 10. Mr. Finch; Scout's dad

_____ 11. The judge for Tom's trial

_____ 12. Preconceived idea

_____ 13. Mrs. Merriweather's ---- circle

_____ 14. To Kill A -----

_____ 15. Tom

_____ 16. 12 who decide

_____ 17. Walter

_____ 18. Cal's boy

_____ 19. Cal rubbed Walter's nose in it

_____ 20. Where Boo spent most of his time

To Kill A Mockingbird Fill In The Blank 3 Answer Key

JACK	1. Atticus's brother
COURTROOM	2. Where trials take place
WALTER	3. Boy Cunningham
MAUDIE	4. Neighbor who liked the children & made cakes
READ	5. Jem had to do it for Mrs. Dubose
ARM	6. Tom's left one had been cut off
AUTHOR	7. Harper Lee
ALEXANDRA	8. Atticus's sister
KILL	9. To end the life of something
ATTICUS	10. Mr. Finch; Scout's dad
TAYLOR	11. The judge for Tom's trial
PREJUDICE	12. Preconceived idea
MISSIONARY	13. Mrs. Merriweather's ---- circle
MOCKINGBIRD	14. To Kill A -----
ROBINSON	15. Tom
JURY	16. 12 who decide
CUNNINGHAM	17. Walter
ZEEBO	18. Cal's boy
DIRT	19. Cal rubbed Walter's nose in it
INSIDE	20. Where Boo spent most of his time

To Kill A Mockingbird Fill In The Blank 4

_____ 1. Miss Fisher's work place

_____ 2. Miss Maudie's flowers

_____ 3. Instrument that killed Bob Ewell

_____ 4. Charles Baker Harris

_____ 5. What Scout wanted Boo to be

_____ 6. Scout and Jem went to Calpurnia's

_____ 7. Tom was shot while trying to ----

_____ 8. What Burris Ewell had to go home and wash out

_____ 9. The Cunninghams didn't have the proper --- to suit Alexandra

_____ 10. Mr. Deas; He escorted Helen

_____ 11. Object of the Radley Games

_____ 12. Two of these carved from soap were in the tree

_____ 13. Miss Fisher

_____ 14. Harper Lee

_____ 15. Process by which innocence or guilt is determined

_____ 16. Gossipy neighbor

_____ 17. Miss Maudie made little ones for the children

_____ 18. Scout's pageant costume

_____ 19. Atticus shot a mad one

_____ 20. Mr. Finch; Scout's dad

To Kill A Mockingbird Fill In The Blank 4 Answer Key

SCHOOL	1. Miss Fisher's work place
AZALEAS	2. Miss Maudie's flowers
KNIFE	3. Instrument that killed Bob Ewell
DILL	4. Charles Baker Harris
NORMAL	5. What Scout wanted Boo to be
CHURCH	6. Scout and Jem went to Calpurnia's
ESCAPE	7. Tom was shot while trying to ----
COOTIES	8. What Burris Ewell had to go home and wash out
BACKGROUND	9. The Cunninghams didn't have the proper --- to suit Alexandra
LINK	10. Mr. Deas; He escorted Helen
BOO	11. Object of the Radley Games
FIGURES	12. Two of these carved from soap were in the tree
CAROLINE	13. Miss Fisher
AUTHOR	14. Harper Lee
TRIAL	15. Process by which innocence or guilt is determined
CRAWFORD	16. Gossipy neighbor
CAKES	17. Miss Maudie made little ones for the children
HAM	18. Scout's pageant costume
DOG	19. Atticus shot a mad one
ATTICUS	20. Mr. Finch; Scout's dad

Copyrighted

To Kill A Mockingbird Matching 1

___ 1. FIRE   A. Cal's boy
___ 2. FINCH   B. Scout's pageant costume
___ 3. CEMENT   C. The hiding place for trinkets
___ 4. SHOT   D. Scout, Jem and Dill, for example; children
___ 5. NORMAL   E. It plugged up the tree hole
___ 6. PULITZER   F. Two of these carved from soap were in the tree
___ 7. BOO   G. Cal rubbed Walter's nose in it
___ 8. KIDS   H. Miss Maudie made little ones for the children
___ 9. CAKES   I. She was allegedly raped
___10. MOB   J. Dolphus
___11. JEM   K. Indian head ones were in the tree
___12. LAWYER   L. Process by which innocence or guilt is determined
___13. PANTS   M. Atticus's occupation
___14. RAYMOND   N. What Jem did after he heard the verdict
___15. COMPANY   O. Scout, Jem or Atticus, for example
___16. ZEEBO   P. It destroyed Miss Maudie's home
___17. CRIED   Q. They wanted to inflict their own justice on Tom
___18. TREE   R. 'He ain't ---, Cal, he's a Cunningham.'
___19. TRIAL   S. Tom was --- trying to escape
___20. MAYELLA   T. Harper Lee
___21. HAM   U. What Scout wanted Boo to be
___22. AUTHOR   V. Scout's brother
___23. DIRT   W. Harper Lee won the --- Prize for Mockingbird
___24. PENNIES   X. Object of the Radley Games
___25. FIGURES   Y. Jem's got caught on the fence

To Kill A Mockingbird Matching 1 Answer Key

P - 1. FIRE	A. Cal's boy
O - 2. FINCH	B. Scout's pageant costume
E - 3. CEMENT	C. The hiding place for trinkets
S - 4. SHOT	D. Scout, Jem and Dill, for example; children
U - 5. NORMAL	E. It plugged up the tree hole
W - 6. PULITZER	F. Two of these carved from soap were in the tree
X - 7. BOO	G. Cal rubbed Walter's nose in it
D - 8. KIDS	H. Miss Maudie made little ones for the children
H - 9. CAKES	I. She was allegedly raped
Q -10. MOB	J. Dolphus
V -11. JEM	K. Indian head ones were in the tree
M -12. LAWYER	L. Process by which innocence or guilt is determined
Y -13. PANTS	M. Atticus's occupation
J -14. RAYMOND	N. What Jem did after he heard the verdict
R -15. COMPANY	O. Scout, Jem or Atticus, for example
A -16. ZEEBO	P. It destroyed Miss Maudie's home
N -17. CRIED	Q. They wanted to inflict their own justice on Tom
C -18. TREE	R. 'He ain't ---, Cal, he's a Cunningham.'
L -19. TRIAL	S. Tom was --- trying to escape
I -20. MAYELLA	T. Harper Lee
B -21. HAM	U. What Scout wanted Boo to be
T -22. AUTHOR	V. Scout's brother
G -23. DIRT	W. Harper Lee won the --- Prize for Mockingbird
K -24. PENNIES	X. Object of the Radley Games
F -25. FIGURES	Y. Jem's got caught on the fence

Copyrighted

To Kill A Mockingbird Matching 2

___ 1. JURY   A. Time of year when Dill visited usually
___ 2. PENNIES   B. Jem had to do it for Mrs. Dubose
___ 3. BALCONY   C. Walter
___ 4. SUMMER   D. Indian head ones were in the tree
___ 5. TO   E. She was allegedly raped
___ 6. GAME   F. They wanted to inflict their own justice on Tom
___ 7. MOB   G. Harper; author
___ 8. TATE   H. Heck; the sheriff
___ 9. PANTS   I. The Jacobs boy
___ 10. CUNNINGHAM   J. To end the life of something
___ 11. MISSIONARY   K. Preconceived idea
___ 12. CALPURNIA   L. What Burris Ewell had to go home and wash out
___ 13. CECIL   M. -- Kill A Mockingbird
___ 14. MOCKINGBIRD   N. Finch housekeeper, cook & nanny
___ 15. COOTIES   O. The kids played the Boo Radley ----
___ 16. KILL   P. Mrs. Merriweather's ---- circle
___ 17. BACKGROUND   Q. Place from which Scout watched the trial
___ 18. PREJUDICE   R. Jem's got caught on the fence
___ 19. CEMENT   S. Word to describe Miss Gates
___ 20. HYPOCRITE   T. Dill's initials
___ 21. MAYELLA   U. To Kill A -----
___ 22. CBH   V. The Cunninghams didn't have the proper --- to suit Alexandra
___ 23. LEE   W. 12 who decide
___ 24. LAWYER   X. It plugged up the tree hole
___ 25. READ   Y. Atticus's occupation

To Kill A Mockingbird Matching 2 Answer Key

W - 1.	JURY	A. Time of year when Dill visited usually
D - 2.	PENNIES	B. Jem had to do it for Mrs. Dubose
Q - 3.	BALCONY	C. Walter
A - 4.	SUMMER	D. Indian head ones were in the tree
M - 5.	TO	E. She was allegedly raped
O - 6.	GAME	F. They wanted to inflict their own justice on Tom
F - 7.	MOB	G. Harper; author
H - 8.	TATE	H. Heck; the sheriff
R - 9.	PANTS	I. The Jacobs boy
C - 10.	CUNNINGHAM	J. To end the life of something
P - 11.	MISSIONARY	K. Preconceived idea
N - 12.	CALPURNIA	L. What Burris Ewell had to go home and wash out
I - 13.	CECIL	M. -- Kill A Mockingbird
U - 14.	MOCKINGBIRD	N. Finch housekeeper, cook & nanny
L - 15.	COOTIES	O. The kids played the Boo Radley ----
J - 16.	KILL	P. Mrs. Merriweather's ---- circle
V - 17.	BACKGROUND	Q. Place from which Scout watched the trial
K - 18.	PREJUDICE	R. Jem's got caught on the fence
X - 19.	CEMENT	S. Word to describe Miss Gates
S - 20.	HYPOCRITE	T. Dill's initials
E - 21.	MAYELLA	U. To Kill A -----
T - 22.	CBH	V. The Cunninghams didn't have the proper --- to suit Alexandra
G - 23.	LEE	W. 12 who decide
Y - 24.	LAWYER	X. It plugged up the tree hole
B - 25.	READ	Y. Atticus's occupation

To Kill A Mockingbird Matching 3

___ 1. CALPURNIA   A. Object found in the tree
___ 2. COURTROOM   B. Mayella's right side had lots of these
___ 3. EWELL   C. Rev. at Cal's church
___ 4. PENNIES   D. Tom
___ 5. PANTS   E. Miss Fisher's work place
___ 6. TO   F. Gossipy neighbor
___ 7. HAM   G. Boy Cunningham
___ 8. TATE   H. It plugged up the tree hole
___ 9. BRUISES   I. Instrument that killed Bob Ewell
___10. EDUCATION   J. Jem's got caught on the fence
___11. KNIFE   K. Tom's left one had been cut off
___12. PAGEANT   L. Harper; author
___13. LEE   M. Atticus's brother
___14. ROBINSON   N. What one gets at school
___15. ARM   O. Finch housekeeper, cook & nanny
___16. WALTER   P. Heck; the sheriff
___17. SHOT   Q. Where trials take place
___18. ALEXANDRA   R. Bob or Mayella
___19. GUM   S. Indian head ones were in the tree
___20. SYKES   T. Atticus's sister
___21. READ   U. -- Kill A Mockingbird
___22. SCHOOL   V. Tom was --- trying to escape
___23. CEMENT   W. Scout made a late entry and ruined it
___24. CRAWFORD   X. Scout's pageant costume
___25. JACK   Y. Jem had to do it for Mrs. Dubose

To Kill A Mockingbird Matching 3 Answer Key

O - 1.	CALPURNIA	A. Object found in the tree
Q - 2.	COURTROOM	B. Mayella's right side had lots of these
R - 3.	EWELL	C. Rev. at Cal's church
S - 4.	PENNIES	D. Tom
J - 5.	PANTS	E. Miss Fisher's work place
U - 6.	TO	F. Gossipy neighbor
X - 7.	HAM	G. Boy Cunningham
P - 8.	TATE	H. It plugged up the tree hole
B - 9.	BRUISES	I. Instrument that killed Bob Ewell
N - 10.	EDUCATION	J. Jem's got caught on the fence
I - 11.	KNIFE	K. Tom's left one had been cut off
W - 12.	PAGEANT	L. Harper; author
L - 13.	LEE	M. Atticus's brother
D - 14.	ROBINSON	N. What one gets at school
K - 15.	ARM	O. Finch housekeeper, cook & nanny
G - 16.	WALTER	P. Heck; the sheriff
V - 17.	SHOT	Q. Where trials take place
T - 18.	ALEXANDRA	R. Bob or Mayella
A - 19.	GUM	S. Indian head ones were in the tree
C - 20.	SYKES	T. Atticus's sister
Y - 21.	READ	U. -- Kill A Mockingbird
E - 22.	SCHOOL	V. Tom was --- trying to escape
H - 23.	CEMENT	W. Scout made a late entry and ruined it
F - 24.	CRAWFORD	X. Scout's pageant costume
M - 25.	JACK	Y. Jem had to do it for Mrs. Dubose

To Kill A Mockingbird Matching 4

___ 1. INSIDE A. It destroyed Miss Maudie's home
___ 2. NORMAL B. Time of year when Dill visited usually
___ 3. PAGEANT C. Scout made a late entry and ruined it
___ 4. MAYELLA D. Charles Baker Harris
___ 5. BACKGROUND E. Atticus's sister
___ 6. DUBOSE F. Scout's brother
___ 7. PANTS G. Where Boo spent most of his time
___ 8. AZALEAS H. 'He ain't ---, Cal, he's a Cunningham.'
___ 9. ALEXANDRA I. Jem's got caught on the fence
___ 10. GAME J. Tom was --- trying to escape
___ 11. HELEN K. The Cunninghams didn't have the proper --- to suit Alexandra
___ 12. DILL L. Miss Maudie's flowers
___ 13. JACK M. Harper Lee
___ 14. LEE N. Atticus's brother
___ 15. LINK O. Jem chopped the tops off her camellia bushes
___ 16. SHOT P. Mr. Cunningham had this; he would not take charity
___ 17. JEM Q. The kids played the Boo Radley ----
___ 18. PRIDE R. Tom's left one had been cut off
___ 19. SUMMER S. The Jacobs boy
___ 20. CECIL T. She was allegedly raped
___ 21. LULA U. Mr. Deas; He escorted Helen
___ 22. AUTHOR V. What Scout wanted Boo to be
___ 23. FIRE W. Harper; author
___ 24. COMPANY X. Mrs. Robinson
___ 25. ARM Y. Woman at Cal's church who made Scout feel unwelcome

To Kill A Mockingbird Matching 4 Answer Key

G - 1. INSIDE	A.	It destroyed Miss Maudie's home
V - 2. NORMAL	B.	Time of year when Dill visited usually
C - 3. PAGEANT	C.	Scout made a late entry and ruined it
T - 4. MAYELLA	D.	Charles Baker Harris
K - 5. BACKGROUND	E.	Atticus's sister
O - 6. DUBOSE	F.	Scout's brother
I - 7. PANTS	G.	Where Boo spent most of his time
L - 8. AZALEAS	H.	'He ain't ---, Cal, he's a Cunningham.'
E - 9. ALEXANDRA	I.	Jem's got caught on the fence
Q -10. GAME	J.	Tom was --- trying to escape
X -11. HELEN	K.	The Cunninghams didn't have the proper --- to suit Alexandra
D -12. DILL	L.	Miss Maudie's flowers
N -13. JACK	M.	Harper Lee
W -14. LEE	N.	Atticus's brother
U -15. LINK	O.	Jem chopped the tops off her camellia bushes
J -16. SHOT	P.	Mr. Cunningham had this; he would not take charity
F -17. JEM	Q.	The kids played the Boo Radley ----
P -18. PRIDE	R.	Tom's left one had been cut off
B -19. SUMMER	S.	The Jacobs boy
S -20. CECIL	T.	She was allegedly raped
Y -21. LULA	U.	Mr. Deas; He escorted Helen
M -22. AUTHOR	V.	What Scout wanted Boo to be
A -23. FIRE	W.	Harper; author
H -24. COMPANY	X.	Mrs. Robinson
R -25. ARM	Y.	Woman at Cal's church who made Scout feel unwelcome

To Kill A Mockingbird Magic Squares 1

Match the definition with the vocabulary word. Put your answers in the magic squares below. When your answers are correct, all columns and rows will add to the same number.

A. JEM
B. BRUISES
C. TAYLOR
D. DILL
E. KILL
F. MISSIONARY
G. SYKES
H. GUM
I. KNIFE
J. EVIDENCE
K. BALCONY
L. LEE
M. CHURCH
N. FIGURES
O. PANTS
P. MAYCOMB

1. Jem's got caught on the fence
2. Material proof
3. Object found in the tree
4. Scout's brother
5. Charles Baker Harris
6. To end the life of something
7. Place from which Scout watched the trial
8. Two of these carved from soap were in the tree
9. Mrs. Merriweather's ---- circle
10. The judge for Tom's trial
11. Scout and Jem went to Calpurnia's
12. Harper; author
13. Instrument that killed Bob Ewell
14. Name of the town and county
15. Mayella's right side had lots of these
16. Rev. at Cal's church

A=	B=	C=	D=
E=	F=	G=	H=
I=	J=	K=	L=
M=	N=	O=	P=

To Kill A Mockingbird Magic Squares 1 Answer Key

Match the definition with the vocabulary word. Put your answers in the magic squares below. When your answers are correct, all columns and rows will add to the same number.

A. JEM
B. BRUISES
C. TAYLOR
D. DILL
E. KILL
F. MISSIONARY
G. SYKES
H. GUM
I. KNIFE
J. EVIDENCE
K. BALCONY
L. LEE
M. CHURCH
N. FIGURES
O. PANTS
P. MAYCOMB

1. Jem's got caught on the fence
2. Material proof
3. Object found in the tree
4. Scout's brother
5. Charles Baker Harris
6. To end the life of something
7. Place from which Scout watched the trial
8. Two of these carved from soap were in the tree
9. Mrs. Merriweather's ---- circle
10. The judge for Tom's trial
11. Scout and Jem went to Calpurnia's
12. Harper; author
13. Instrument that killed Bob Ewell
14. Name of the town and county
15. Mayella's right side had lots of these
16. Rev. at Cal's church

A=4	B=15	C=10	D=5
E=6	F=9	G=16	H=3
I=13	J=2	K=7	L=12
M=11	N=8	O=1	P=14

To Kill A Mockingbird Magic Squares 2

Match the definition with the vocabulary word. Put your answers in the magic squares below. When your answers are correct, all columns and rows will add to the same number.

A. SCHOOL
B. KILL
C. TATE
D. HELEN
E. LAWYER
F. BACKGROUND
G. CAKES
H. COMPANY
I. SYKES
J. SUMMER
K. PAGEANT
L. DOG
M. CRIED
N. MOB
O. JEM
P. ZEEBO

1. 'He ain't ---, Cal, he's a Cunningham.'
2. What Jem did after he heard the verdict
3. To end the life of something
4. Scout made a late entry and ruined it
5. Time of year when Dill visited usually
6. Heck; the sheriff
7. Cal's boy
8. Atticus's occupation
9. Scout's brother
10. The Cunninghams didn't have the proper --- to suit Alexandra
11. Rev. at Cal's church
12. Mrs. Robinson
13. Miss Fisher's work place
14. Atticus shot a mad one
15. Miss Maudie made little ones for the children
16. They wanted to inflict their own justice on Tom

A=	B=	C=	D=
E=	F=	G=	H=
I=	J=	K=	L=
M=	N=	O=	P=

To Kill A Mockingbird Magic Squares 2 Answer Key

Match the definition with the vocabulary word. Put your answers in the magic squares below. When your answers are correct, all columns and rows will add to the same number.

A. SCHOOL
B. KILL
C. TATE
D. HELEN
E. LAWYER
F. BACKGROUND
G. CAKES
H. COMPANY
I. SYKES
J. SUMMER
K. PAGEANT
L. DOG
M. CRIED
N. MOB
O. JEM
P. ZEEBO

1. 'He ain't ---, Cal, he's a Cunningham.'
2. What Jem did after he heard the verdict
3. To end the life of something
4. Scout made a late entry and ruined it
5. Time of year when Dill visited usually
6. Heck; the sheriff
7. Cal's boy
8. Atticus's occupation
9. Scout's brother
10. The Cunninghams didn't have the proper --- to suit Alexandra
11. Rev. at Cal's church
12. Mrs. Robinson
13. Miss Fisher's work place
14. Atticus shot a mad one
15. Miss Maudie made little ones for the children
16. They wanted to inflict their own justice on Tom

A=13	B=3	C=6	D=12
E=8	F=10	G=15	H=1
I=11	J=5	K=4	L=14
M=2	N=16	O=9	P=7

To Kill A Mockingbird Magic Squares 3

Match the definition with the vocabulary word. Put your answers in the magic squares below. When your answers are correct, all columns and rows will add to the same number.

A. KNIFE
B. CBH
C. FIRE
D. COURTROOM
E. EVIDENCE
F. MOCKINGBIRD
G. SHOT
H. PAGEANT
I. CRIED
J. BACKGROUND
K. PREJUDICE
L. JEM
M. CRAWFORD
N. LINK
O. SCHOOL
P. KIDS

1. Gossipy neighbor
2. To Kill A -----
3. Scout made a late entry and ruined it
4. Miss Fisher's work place
5. Scout's brother
6. It destroyed Miss Maudie's home
7. Instrument that killed Bob Ewell
8. The Cunninghams didn't have the proper --- to suit Alexandra
9. Preconceived idea
10. Where trials take place
11. Dill's initials
12. What Jem did after he heard the verdict
13. Mr. Deas; He escorted Helen
14. Material proof
15. Tom was --- trying to escape
16. Scout, Jem and Dill, for example; children

A=	B=	C=	D=
E=	F=	G=	H=
I=	J=	K=	L=
M=	N=	O=	P=

To Kill A Mockingbird Magic Squares 3 Answer Key

Match the definition with the vocabulary word. Put your answers in the magic squares below. When your answers are correct, all columns and rows will add to the same number.

A. KNIFE
B. CBH
C. FIRE
D. COURTROOM
E. EVIDENCE
F. MOCKINGBIRD
G. SHOT
H. PAGEANT
I. CRIED
J. BACKGROUND
K. PREJUDICE
L. JEM
M. CRAWFORD
N. LINK
O. SCHOOL
P. KIDS

1. Gossipy neighbor
2. To Kill A -----
3. Scout made a late entry and ruined it
4. Miss Fisher's work place
5. Scout's brother
6. It destroyed Miss Maudie's home
7. Instrument that killed Bob Ewell
8. The Cunninghams didn't have the proper --- to suit Alexandra
9. Preconceived idea
10. Where trials take place
11. Dill's initials
12. What Jem did after he heard the verdict
13. Mr. Deas; He escorted Helen
14. Material proof
15. Tom was --- trying to escape
16. Scout, Jem and Dill, for example; children

A=7	B=11	C=6	D=10
E=14	F=2	G=15	H=3
I=12	J=8	K=9	L=5
M=1	N=13	O=4	P=16

To Kill A Mockingbird Magic Squares 4

Match the definition with the vocabulary word. Put your answers in the magic squares below. When your answers are correct, all columns and rows will add to the same number.

A. ESCAPE
B. PRIDE
C. DOG
D. MOB
E. CRAWFORD
F. KILL
G. CALPURNIA
H. RAYMOND
I. CRIED
J. DUBOSE
K. CHURCH
L. AUTHOR
M. DIRT
N. TAYLOR
O. DILL
P. PAGEANT

1. Dolphus
2. Tom was shot while trying to ----
3. Mr. Cunningham had this; he would not take charity
4. Finch housekeeper, cook & nanny
5. Jem chopped the tops off her camellia bushes
6. Charles Baker Harris
7. Scout made a late entry and ruined it
8. What Jem did after he heard the verdict
9. Scout and Jem went to Calpurnia's
10. The judge for Tom's trial
11. Cal rubbed Walter's nose in it
12. Harper Lee
13. Gossipy neighbor
14. They wanted to inflict their own justice on Tom
15. Atticus shot a mad one
16. To end the life of something

A= 2	B= 3	C= 15	D= 14
E= 13	F= 16	G= 4	H= 1
I= 8	J= 5	K= 9	L= 12
M= 11	N= 10	O= 6	P= 7

To Kill A Mockingbird Magic Squares 4 Answer Key

Match the definition with the vocabulary word. Put your answers in the magic squares below. When your answers are correct, all columns and rows will add to the same number.

A. ESCAPE
B. PRIDE
C. DOG
D. MOB
E. CRAWFORD
F. KILL
G. CALPURNIA
H. RAYMOND
I. CRIED
J. DUBOSE
K. CHURCH
L. AUTHOR
M. DIRT
N. TAYLOR
O. DILL
P. PAGEANT

1. Dolphus
2. Tom was shot while trying to ----
3. Mr. Cunningham had this; he would not take charity
4. Finch housekeeper, cook & nanny
5. Jem chopped the tops off her camellia bushes
6. Charles Baker Harris
7. Scout made a late entry and ruined it
8. What Jem did after he heard the verdict
9. Scout and Jem went to Calpurnia's
10. The judge for Tom's trial
11. Cal rubbed Walter's nose in it
12. Harper Lee
13. Gossipy neighbor
14. They wanted to inflict their own justice on Tom
15. Atticus shot a mad one
16. To end the life of something

A=2	B=3	C=15	D=14
E=13	F=16	G=4	H=1
I=8	J=5	K=9	L=12
M=11	N=10	O=6	P=7

To Kill A Mockingbird Word Search 1

```
M E D U C A T I O N A P L U L A
A M W Z B E N Z B A L R R I T D
Y O C K H S M E O R E E A I Y T
C O T I E S E O M X J N M D J
O R C D R L W B N Y A U O O I E
M T E I L D A O C T N D R B R N
B R F I R L L A L D I M M T Q
C U K L E I T I L I R C A I A T
K O L Y M B E C P N A E L S T D
C C W R A G R E U K Y B J S E K
H A M U U N T C R J E V G I S Q
L U L J D I A N N Q E S Z O H H
G R G E I K B G I D V M C N O W
L L E W E C W M A Y E L L A T M
K I D S F O R E M M U S B R P M
F I N C H M R D O G E T O Y N E
```

-- Kill A Mockingbird (2)
12 who decide (4)
Atticus shot a mad one (3)
Atticus's occupation (6)
Atticus's sister (9)
Bob or Mayella (5)
Boy Cunningham (6)
Cal rubbed Walter's nose in it (4)
Cal's boy (5)
Charles Baker Harris (4)
Dill's initials (3)
Finch housekeeper, cook & nanny (9)
Harper; author (3)
Heck; the sheriff (4)
It destroyed Miss Maudie's home (4)
It housed Tom Robinson while he waited for a trial (4)
It plugged up the tree hole (6)
Jem had to do it for Mrs. Dubose (4)
Jem pushed Scout into the Radley's --- (4)
Miss Maudie made little ones for the children (5)
Mr. Cunningham had this; he would not take charity (5)
Mr. Deas; He escorted Helen (4)
Mrs. Merriweather's ---- circle (10)
Name of the town and county (7)
Neighbor who liked the children & made cakes (6)
Object found in the tree (3)
Object of the Radley Games (3)
Preconceived idea (9)
Scout's brother (3)
Scout's pageant costume (3)
Scout, Jem and Dill, for example; children (4)
Scout, Jem or Atticus, for example (5)
She was allegedly raped (7)
The Jacobs boy (5)
The kids played the Boo Radley ---- (4)
They wanted to inflict their own justice on Tom (3)
Time of year when Dill visited usually (6)
To Kill A ----- (11)
To end the life of something (4)
Tom was --- trying to escape (4)
Tom was shot while trying to ---- (6)
Tom's left one had been cut off (3)
What Burris Ewell had to go home and wash out (7)
What Scout wanted Boo to be (6)
What one gets at school (9)
Where Boo spent most of his time (6)
Where trials take place (9)
Woman at Cal's church who made Scout feel unwelcome (4)

To Kill A Mockingbird Word Search 1 Answer Key

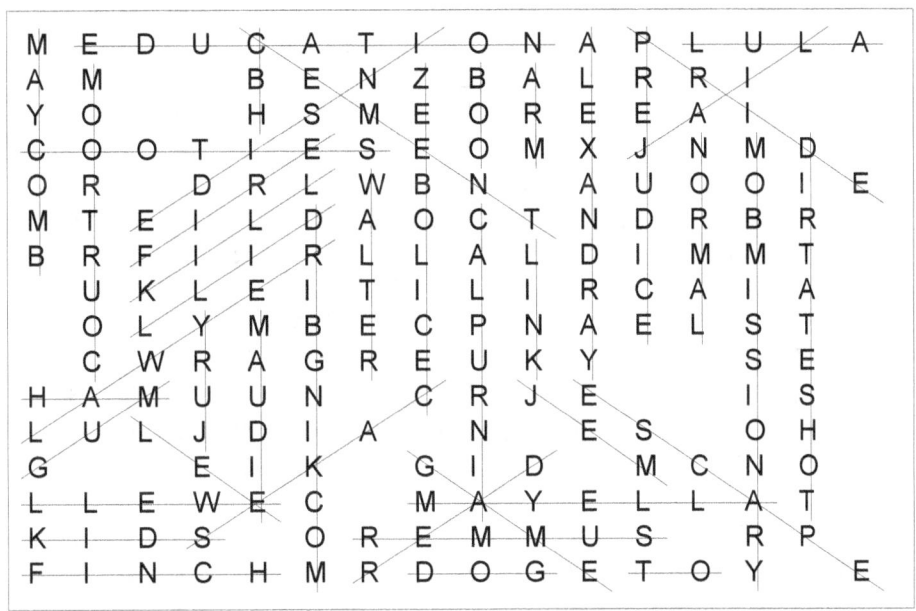

-- Kill A Mockingbird (2)
12 who decide (4)
Atticus shot a mad one (3)
Atticus's occupation (6)
Atticus's sister (9)
Bob or Mayella (5)
Boy Cunningham (6)
Cal rubbed Walter's nose in it (4)
Cal's boy (5)
Charles Baker Harris (4)
Dill's initials (3)
Finch housekeeper, cook & nanny (9)
Harper; author (3)
Heck; the sheriff (4)
It destroyed Miss Maudie's home (4)
It housed Tom Robinson while he waited for a trial (4)
It plugged up the tree hole (6)
Jem had to do it for Mrs. Dubose (4)
Jem pushed Scout into the Radley's --- (4)
Miss Maudie made little ones for the children (5)
Mr. Cunningham had this; he would not take charity (5)
Mr. Deas; He escorted Helen (4)
Mrs. Merriweather's ---- circle (10)
Name of the town and county (7)
Neighbor who liked the children & made cakes (6)
Object found in the tree (3)
Object of the Radley Games (3)
Preconceived idea (9)
Scout's brother (3)
Scout's pageant costume (3)
Scout, Jem and Dill, for example; children (4)
Scout, Jem or Atticus, for example (5)
She was allegedly raped (7)
The Jacobs boy (5)
The kids played the Boo Radley ---- (4)
They wanted to inflict their own justice on Tom (3)
Time of year when Dill visited usually (6)
To Kill A ----- (11)
To end the life of something (4)
Tom was --- trying to escape (4)
Tom was shot while trying to ---- (6)
Tom's left one had been cut off (3)
What Burris Ewell had to go home and wash out (7)
What Scout wanted Boo to be (6)
What one gets at school (9)
Where Boo spent most of his time (6)
Where trials take place (9)
Woman at Cal's church who made Scout feel unwelcome (4)

To Kill A Mockingbird Word Search 2

```
B C O U R T R O O M C E C I L S
R O R H E N R B L L E D R R L Z
A M O M T A R E D L V I I O I Y
V K R L L E X E E O R R E B D B
E A X S A G V Z A O G P D I T G
R T X C W A K D H D P H T N U Y
Y A E W Y P T T T F C B N S O E
A Y D D R D U T R N X V E O C R
L L I K U A E R I F H A M N S P
M O E B J C T F D C L N E O L H
A R O X M V A H K U U D C A B H
Y S K C A J T T L N I S M G Y D
E Y I A U N T G I V I R Q A A H
L K D K D G D O E O O F J M R S
L E S E I D U R Y N N R E E D Z
A S M S E N V M A Y C O M B M N
```

-- Kill A Mockingbird (2)
12 who decide (4)
Atticus shot a mad one (3)
Atticus's brother (4)
Atticus's sister (9)
Boy Cunningham (6)
Cal rubbed Walter's nose in it (4)
Cal's boy (5)
Charles Baker Harris (4)
Courage (7)
Harper Lee (6)
Harper; author (3)
Heck; the sheriff (4)
Instrument that killed Bob Ewell (5)
It destroyed Miss Maudie's home (4)
It plugged up the tree hole (6)
Jem chopped the tops off her camellia bushes (6)
Jem had to do it for Mrs. Dubose (4)
Jem pushed Scout into the Radley's --- (4)
Material proof (8)
Miss Maudie made little ones for the children (5)
Mr. Cunningham had this; he would not take charity (5)
Mr. Finch; Scout's dad (7)
Name of the town and county (7)
Narrator (5)

Neighbor who liked the children & made cakes (6)
Object found in the tree (3)
Object of the Radley Games (3)
Rev. at Cal's church (5)
Scout made a late entry and ruined it (7)
Scout's brother (3)
Scout's pageant costume (3)
Scout, Jem and Dill, for example; children (4)
Scout, Jem or Atticus, for example (5)
She was allegedly raped (7)
The Jacobs boy (5)
The hiding place for trinkets (4)
The judge for Tom's trial (6)
The kids played the Boo Radley ---- (4)
They wanted to inflict their own justice on Tom (3)
To end the life of something (4)
Tom (8)
Tom's left one had been cut off (3)
What Jem did after he heard the verdict (5)
What Scout wanted Boo to be (6)
What one gets at school (9)
Where trials take place (9)
Woman at Cal's church who made Scout feel unwelcome (4)

To Kill A Mockingbird Word Search 2 Answer Key

-- Kill A Mockingbird (2)
12 who decide (4)
Atticus shot a mad one (3)
Atticus's brother (4)
Atticus's sister (9)
Boy Cunningham (6)
Cal rubbed Walter's nose in it (4)
Cal's boy (5)
Charles Baker Harris (4)
Courage (7)
Harper Lee (6)
Harper; author (3)
Heck; the sheriff (4)
Instrument that killed Bob Ewell (5)
It destroyed Miss Maudie's home (4)
It plugged up the tree hole (6)
Jem chopped the tops off her camellia bushes (6)
Jem had to do it for Mrs. Dubose (4)
Jem pushed Scout into the Radley's --- (4)
Material proof (8)
Miss Maudie made little ones for the children (5)
Mr. Cunningham had this; he would not take charity (5)
Mr. Finch; Scout's dad (7)
Name of the town and county (7)
Narrator (5)

Neighbor who liked the children & made cakes (6)
Object found in the tree (3)
Object of the Radley Games (3)
Rev. at Cal's church (5)
Scout made a late entry and ruined it (7)
Scout's brother (3)
Scout's pageant costume (3)
Scout, Jem and Dill, for example; children (4)
Scout, Jem or Atticus, for example (5)
She was allegedly raped (7)
The Jacobs boy (5)
The hiding place for trinkets (4)
The judge for Tom's trial (6)
The kids played the Boo Radley ---- (4)
They wanted to inflict their own justice on Tom (3)
To end the life of something (4)
Tom (8)
Tom's left one had been cut off (3)
What Jem did after he heard the verdict (5)
What Scout wanted Boo to be (6)
What one gets at school (9)
Where trials take place (9)
Woman at Cal's church who made Scout feel unwelcome (4)

To Kill A Mockingbird Word Search 3

```
T K I D S S L T L J U R Y A R D
D A T C T C I U H A E L E N C
I B T R P A N O Z W H Q I L R X
R O I E K K O C B F Y C I T L
T A S Y K E S S P R I D E T N Y
L G V H M E S U F E A D C R S W
G G R A O C Z M V M J W L I K
M U G M I T L S P M A A F T D V
B M F T F I N C H U C L I O E L
L A T T G P A N T S L E U L R T
E L L I D M H Y W M I M L R Y D
D W E C L O O H C S A A T E A K
Z E E B O R F I R E G L U Z N C
L O M L G N X M N E B V T D E T
P O A L L Y Y C O J A C K E I R
C B H J E M E S O B U D O G R E
```

ARM	DOG	JEM	READ
ATTICUS	DUBOSE	JURY	SCHOOL
AUTHOR	EWELL	KIDS	SCOUT
BALCONY	FINCH	KILL	SHOT
BOO	FIRE	LAWYER	SUMMER
CAKES	GAME	LEE	SYKES
CBH	GILMER	LINK	TATE
CECIL	GUM	LULA	TO
CEMENT	HAM	MAUDIE	TREE
CRAWFORD	HELEN	MOB	TRIAL
CRIED	INSIDE	PANTS	WALTER
DILL	JACK	PRIDE	YARD
DIRT	JAIL	PULITZER	ZEEBO

To Kill A Mockingbird Word Search 3 Answer Key

```
T K I D S     L   T   L J U R Y A R D
D A T   T C I U     A H E L E N   C
I   T R   A N O     W   I       R
R O I E E K K C   C       Y C       I
T A S Y K E S S   P R I D E       N
L   H M S U       E E A D C R S
    G R A O C     M   J W L L   I
    U G M I T L   P M A A F   D
B M   T F I N C H U C L I O E
  A   T G P A N T S L E U L R
  E A L L I D   H   W M I M   D
    W E C L O O H C S A A T E A
    Z E E B O R F I R E   L U Z N
    L O M L     N   M   E     T D E T
        O A     L     Y   O J A C K E I R
        C B H J E M E S O B U D O G R E
```

ARM	DOG	JEM	READ
ATTICUS	DUBOSE	JURY	SCHOOL
AUTHOR	EWELL	KIDS	SCOUT
BALCONY	FINCH	KILL	SHOT
BOO	FIRE	LAWYER	SUMMER
CAKES	GAME	LEE	SYKES
CBH	GILMER	LINK	TATE
CECIL	GUM	LULA	TO
CEMENT	HAM	MAUDIE	TREE
CRAWFORD	HELEN	MOB	TRIAL
CRIED	INSIDE	PANTS	WALTER
DILL	JACK	PRIDE	YARD
DIRT	JAIL	PULITZER	ZEEBO

Copyrighted

To Kill A Mockingbird Word Search 4

```
D U B O S E H E L E N C R I E D
V O K R T Y H S I Z L D N P P
M C G R A T K Z A T I I S A G
O R I F R V S E J U T N L G V
B A A I E W E C S A Y K L D E X
L W R N M G K R O M L C Y E A G
Y F M C M O A V Y U O A E N P
L O C H U R C H D I R T J C T F
Q R C S S B Y K I D S T R A I B
A D O S H O T T I T S E R Q C L
K U O B E E Z Z A N Z C J O M K
R E T L A W Y E R T G L H U R T
B K I H Y H K F I Y E B G O R M
O I E T O K I L W H H J I E O Y
O L S S E R U G I F D A E R C L
L L E W E P G A M E F L M M D C
```

ARM	DIRT	JAIL	READ
AUTHOR	DOG	JEM	SCHOOL
BOO	DUBOSE	JURY	SHOT
BRAVERY	EWELL	KIDS	SUMMER
CAKES	FIGURES	KILL	SYKES
CBH	FINCH	LAWYER	TATE
CECIL	FIRE	LEE	TAYLOR
CHURCH	GAME	LINK	TO
COOTIES	GUM	MAUDIE	TREE
COURTROOM	HAM	MOB	TRIAL
CRAWFORD	HELEN	MOCKINGBIRD	WALTER
CRIED	INSIDE	PAGEANT	YARD
DILL	JACK	PULITZER	ZEEBO

To Kill A Mockingbird Word Search 4 Answer Key

```
D U B O S E H E L E N C R I E D
  O R T Y     I I     L D N P
M C G R A K A D T I I N A
O R I F R V S E J U A N L S G
B A J R   E C S A Y K L I E
L W R N M K R O M L C Y D A
    F M C M O A   Y U O A   N
    O C H U R C H D I R T J C T
    R C   S B   K I D S R A
  A D O S H O T T I   S E R C
    U O B E E Z   A N Z C J O M K
  R E T L A W Y E R T G   H U O T
  B K I H       F I   E B G O R M
  O I E T O I L   H J I E O Y
  O L S S E R U G I F D A E R L
  L L E W E P G A M E   L M M D
```

ARM	DIRT	JAIL	READ
AUTHOR	DOG	JEM	SCHOOL
BOO	DUBOSE	JURY	SHOT
BRAVERY	EWELL	KIDS	SUMMER
CAKES	FIGURES	KILL	SYKES
CBH	FINCH	LAWYER	TATE
CECIL	FIRE	LEE	TAYLOR
CHURCH	GAME	LINK	TO
COOTIES	GUM	MAUDIE	TREE
COURTROOM	HAM	MOB	TRIAL
CRAWFORD	HELEN	MOCKINGBIRD	WALTER
CRIED	INSIDE	PAGEANT	YARD
DILL	JACK	PULITZER	ZEEBO

To Kill A Mockingbird Crossword 1

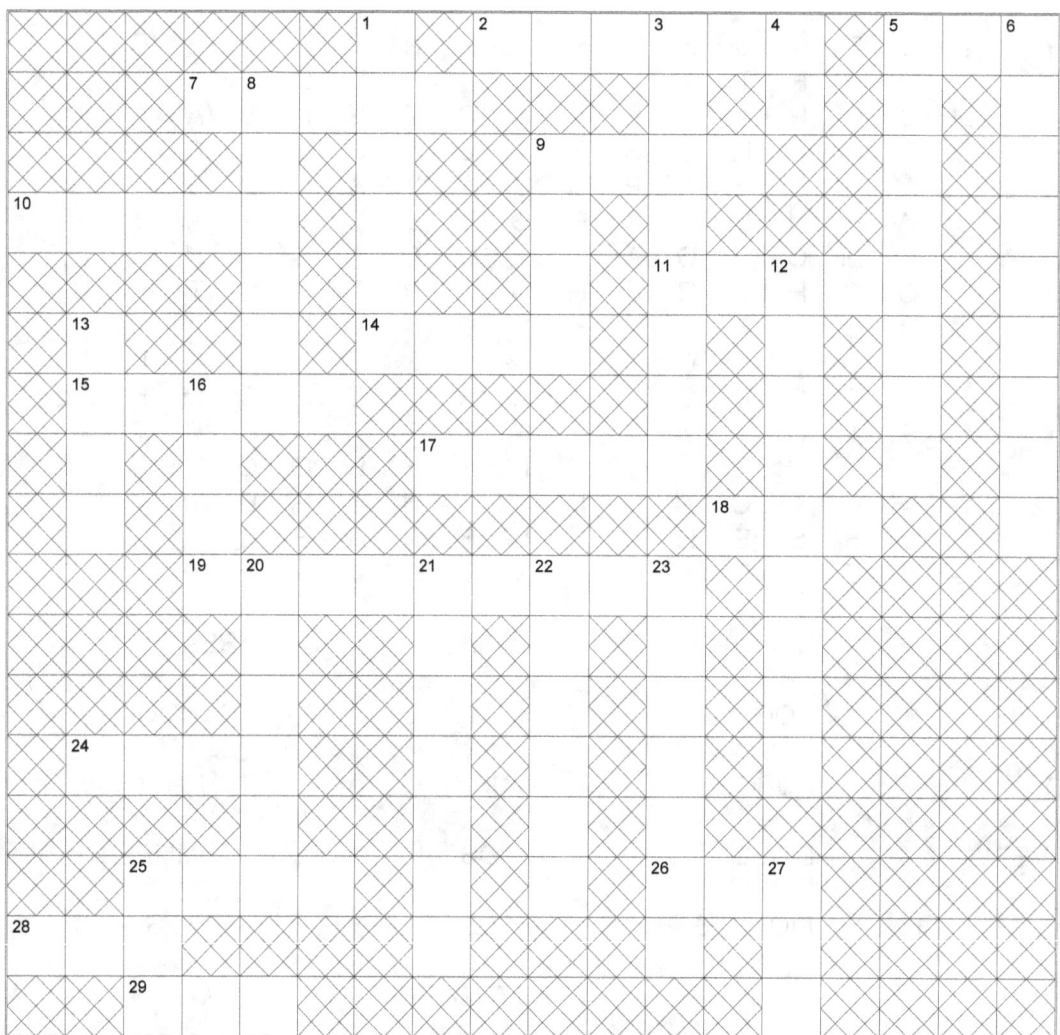

Across
2. It plugged up the tree hole
5. Dill's initials
7. Scout, Jem or Atticus, for example
9. It housed Tom Robinson while he waited for a trial
10. Jem's got caught on the fence
11. Bob or Mayella
14. Mr. Deas; He escorted Helen
15. Mrs. Robinson
17. Mr. Cunningham had this; he would not take charity
18. Scout's pageant costume
19. Atticus's sister
24. 12 who decide
25. Cal rubbed Walter's nose in it
26. Tom's left one had been cut off
28. Object of the Radley Games
29. Object found in the tree

Down
1. Miss Fisher's work place
3. Material proof
4. -- Kill A Mockingbird
5. Miss Fisher
6. Word to describe Miss Gates
8. Where Boo spent most of his time
9. Atticus's brother
12. What one gets at school
13. Tom was --- trying to escape
16. Woman at Cal's church who made Scout feel unwelcome
20. Atticus's occupation
21. Mr. Finch; Scout's dad
22. Jem chopped the tops off her camellia bushes
23. Miss Maudie's flowers
25. Atticus shot a mad one
27. They wanted to inflict their own justice on Tom

To Kill A Mockingbird Crossword 1 Answer Key

					1 S		2 C	E	M	3 E	N	4 T		5 C	B	6 H
		7 F	8 I	N	C	H				V		O		A		Y
			N		H			9 J	A	I	L			R		P
10 P	A	N	T	S		O		A		D				O		O
			I			O		C		11 E	W	12 E	L	L		C
	13 S		D		14 L	I	N	K		N		D		I		R
	15 H	E	16 L	E	N					C		U		N		I
	O		U			17 P	R	I	D	E		C		E		T
	T		L								18 H	A	M			E
			19 A	20 L	E	21 X	A	22 N	D	23 R	A					
				A		T		U		Z		T				
				W		T		B		A		I				
		24 J	U	R	Y			I		O		O				
				E				C		S		N				
			25 D	I	R	T		U		26 E	A	27 R	M			
28 B	O	O						S				O				
			29 G	U	M							B				

Across
2. It plugged up the tree hole
5. Dill's initials
7. Scout, Jem or Atticus, for example
9. It housed Tom Robinson while he waited for a trial
10. Jem's got caught on the fence
11. Bob or Mayella
14. Mr. Deas; He escorted Helen
15. Mrs. Robinson
17. Mr. Cunningham had this; he would not take charity
18. Scout's pageant costume
19. Atticus's sister
24. 12 who decide
25. Cal rubbed Walter's nose in it
26. Tom's left one had been cut off
28. Object of the Radley Games
29. Object found in the tree

Down
1. Miss Fisher's work place
3. Material proof
4. -- Kill A Mockingbird
5. Miss Fisher
6. Word to describe Miss Gates
8. Where Boo spent most of his time
9. Atticus's brother
12. What one gets at school
13. Tom was --- trying to escape
16. Woman at Cal's church who made Scout feel unwelcome
20. Atticus's occupation
21. Mr. Finch; Scout's dad
22. Jem chopped the tops off her camellia bushes
23. Miss Maudie's flowers
25. Atticus shot a mad one
27. They wanted to inflict their own justice on Tom

To Kill A Mockingbird Crossword 2

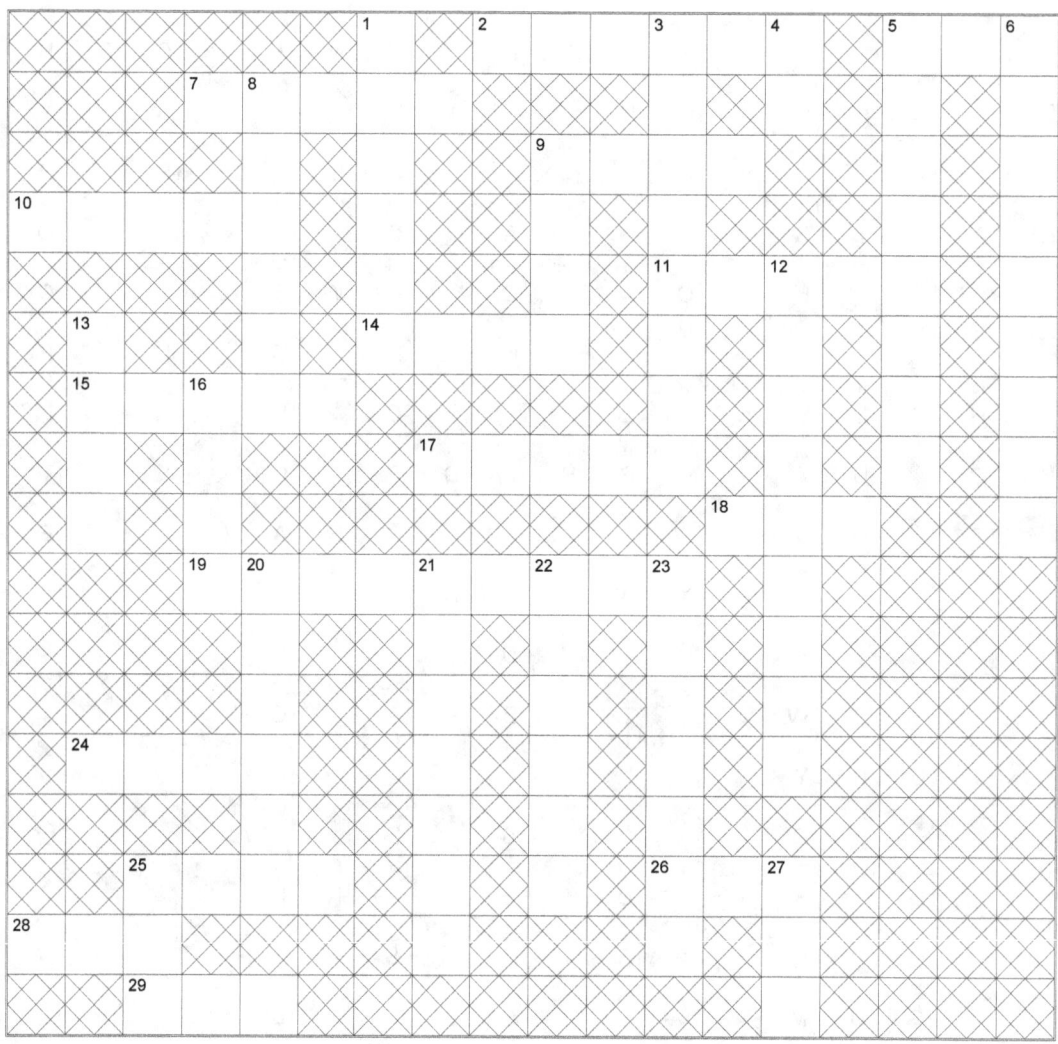

Across
2. It plugged up the tree hole
5. Dill's initials
7. Scout, Jem or Atticus, for example
9. It housed Tom Robinson while he waited for a trial
10. Jem's got caught on the fence
11. Bob or Mayella
14. Mr. Deas; He escorted Helen
15. Mrs. Robinson
17. Mr. Cunningham had this; he would not take charity
18. Scout's pageant costume
19. Atticus's sister
24. 12 who decide
25. Cal rubbed Walter's nose in it
26. Tom's left one had been cut off
28. Object of the Radley Games
29. Object found in the tree

Down
1. Miss Fisher's work place
3. Material proof
4. -- Kill A Mockingbird
5. Miss Fisher
6. Word to describe Miss Gates
8. Where Boo spent most of his time
9. Atticus's brother
12. What one gets at school
13. Tom was --- trying to escape
16. Woman at Cal's church who made Scout feel unwelcome
20. Atticus's occupation
21. Mr. Finch; Scout's dad
22. Jem chopped the tops off her camellia bushes
23. Miss Maudie's flowers
25. Atticus shot a mad one
27. They wanted to inflict their own justice on Tom

To Kill A Mockingbird Crossword 2 Answer Key

Across
2. It plugged up the tree hole
5. Dill's initials
7. Scout, Jem or Atticus, for example
9. It housed Tom Robinson while he waited for a trial
10. Jem's got caught on the fence
11. Bob or Mayella
14. Mr. Deas; He escorted Helen
15. Mrs. Robinson
17. Mr. Cunningham had this; he would not take charity
18. Scout's pageant costume
19. Atticus's sister
24. 12 who decide
25. Cal rubbed Walter's nose in it
26. Tom's left one had been cut off
28. Object of the Radley Games
29. Object found in the tree

Down
1. Miss Fisher's work place
3. Material proof
4. -- Kill A Mockingbird
5. Miss Fisher
6. Word to describe Miss Gates
8. Where Boo spent most of his time
9. Atticus's brother
12. What one gets at school
13. Tom was --- trying to escape
16. Woman at Cal's church who made Scout feel unwelcome
20. Atticus's occupation
21. Mr. Finch; Scout's dad
22. Jem chopped the tops off her camellia bushes
23. Miss Maudie's flowers
25. Atticus shot a mad one
27. They wanted to inflict their own justice on Tom

To Kill A Mockingbird Crossword 3

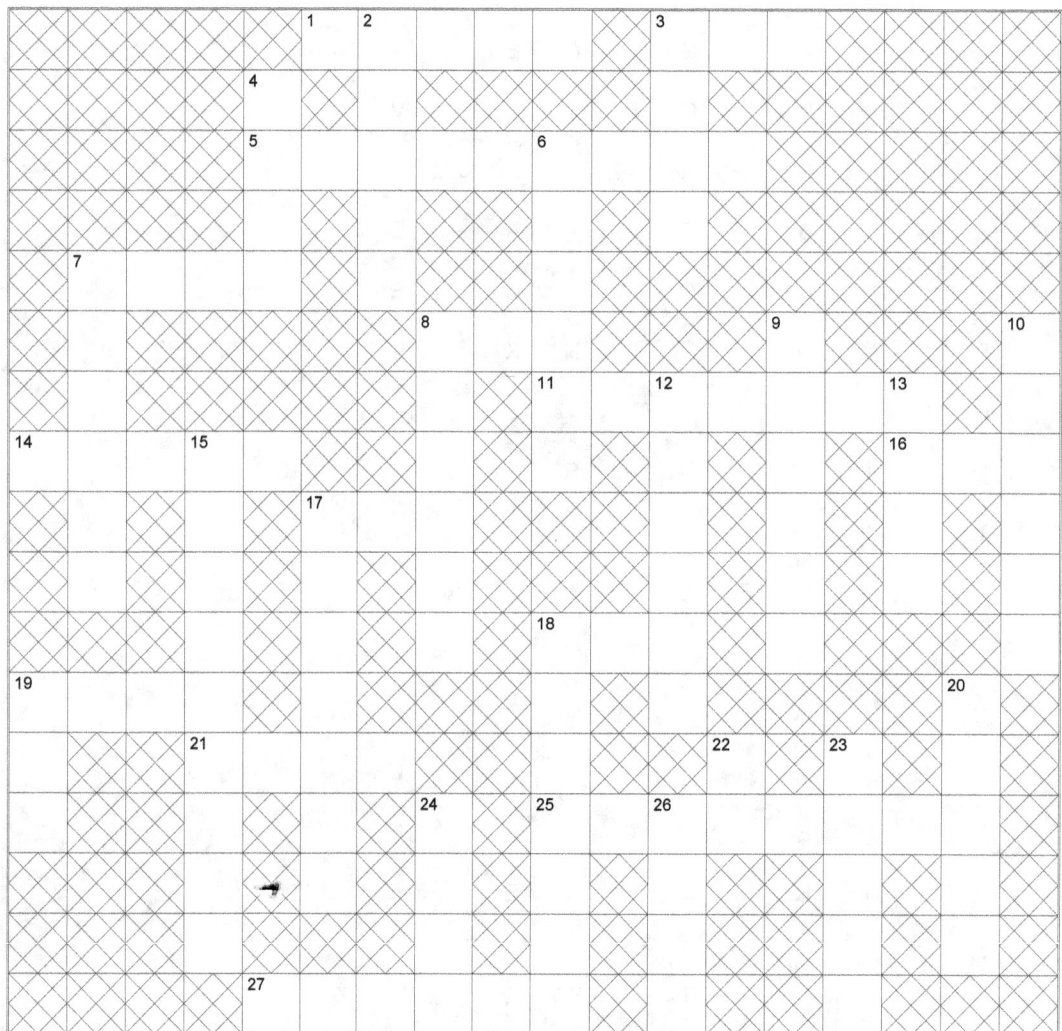

Across
1. Mrs. Robinson
3. Atticus shot a mad one
5. Atticus's sister
7. Mr. Deas; He escorted Helen
8. Object found in the tree
11. Mr. Finch; Scout's dad
14. Rev. at Cal's church
16. Scout's pageant costume
17. Tom's left one had been cut off
18. Object of the Radley Games
19. Woman at Cal's church who made Scout feel unwelcome
21. The hiding place for trinkets
25. Miss Fisher
27. The jury's verdict

Down
2. Bob or Mayella
3. Cal rubbed Walter's nose in it
4. Atticus's brother
6. What Scout wanted Boo to be
7. Atticus's occupation
8. The prosecutor
9. Miss Fisher's work place
10. It plugged up the tree hole
12. The judge for Tom's trial
13. Tom was --- trying to escape
15. What one gets at school
17. Miss Maudie's flowers
18. Place from which Scout watched the trial
19. Harper; author
20. Cal's boy
22. -- Kill A Mockingbird
23. Scout, Jem or Atticus, for example
24. It housed Tom Robinson while he waited for a trial
26. Jem had to do it for Mrs. Dubose

To Kill A Mockingbird Crossword 3 Answer Key

			1 H	2 E	L	E	N		3 D	O	G		
		4 J		W					I				
		5 A	L	E	X	A	6 N	D	R	A			
		C		L			O		T				
	7 L	I	N	K			L						
	A				8 G	U	M			9 S		10 C
	W				I		11 A	12 T	T	I	C	U	13 S	E
14 S	Y	K	15 E	S			L		L		A		H		16 H	A	M
	E		D		17 A	R	M				Y		O		O		E
	R		U		Z		E				L		O		T		N
			C		A		R		18 B	O	O		L				T
19 L	U	L	A		L				A							20 Z
E			21 T	R	E	E			L		22 T		23 F		E
E			I			24 J	25 C	A	26 R	O	L	I	N	E
			O		S		A			O		E		N		B
			N			I			N		A		C		O
				27 G	U	I	L	T	Y		D		H	

Across
1. Mrs. Robinson
3. Atticus shot a mad one
5. Atticus's sister
7. Mr. Deas; He escorted Helen
8. Object found in the tree
11. Mr. Finch; Scout's dad
14. Rev. at Cal's church
16. Scout's pageant costume
17. Tom's left one had been cut off
18. Object of the Radley Games
19. Woman at Cal's church who made Scout feel unwelcome
21. The hiding place for trinkets
25. Miss Fisher
27. The jury's verdict

Down
2. Bob or Mayella
3. Cal rubbed Walter's nose in it
4. Atticus's brother
6. What Scout wanted Boo to be
7. Atticus's occupation
8. The prosecutor
9. Miss Fisher's work place
10. It plugged up the tree hole
12. The judge for Tom's trial
13. Tom was --- trying to escape
15. What one gets at school
17. Miss Maudie's flowers
18. Place from which Scout watched the trial
19. Harper; author
20. Cal's boy
22. -- Kill A Mockingbird
23. Scout, Jem or Atticus, for example
24. It housed Tom Robinson while he waited for a trial
26. Jem had to do it for Mrs. Dubose

To Kill A Mockingbird Crossword 4

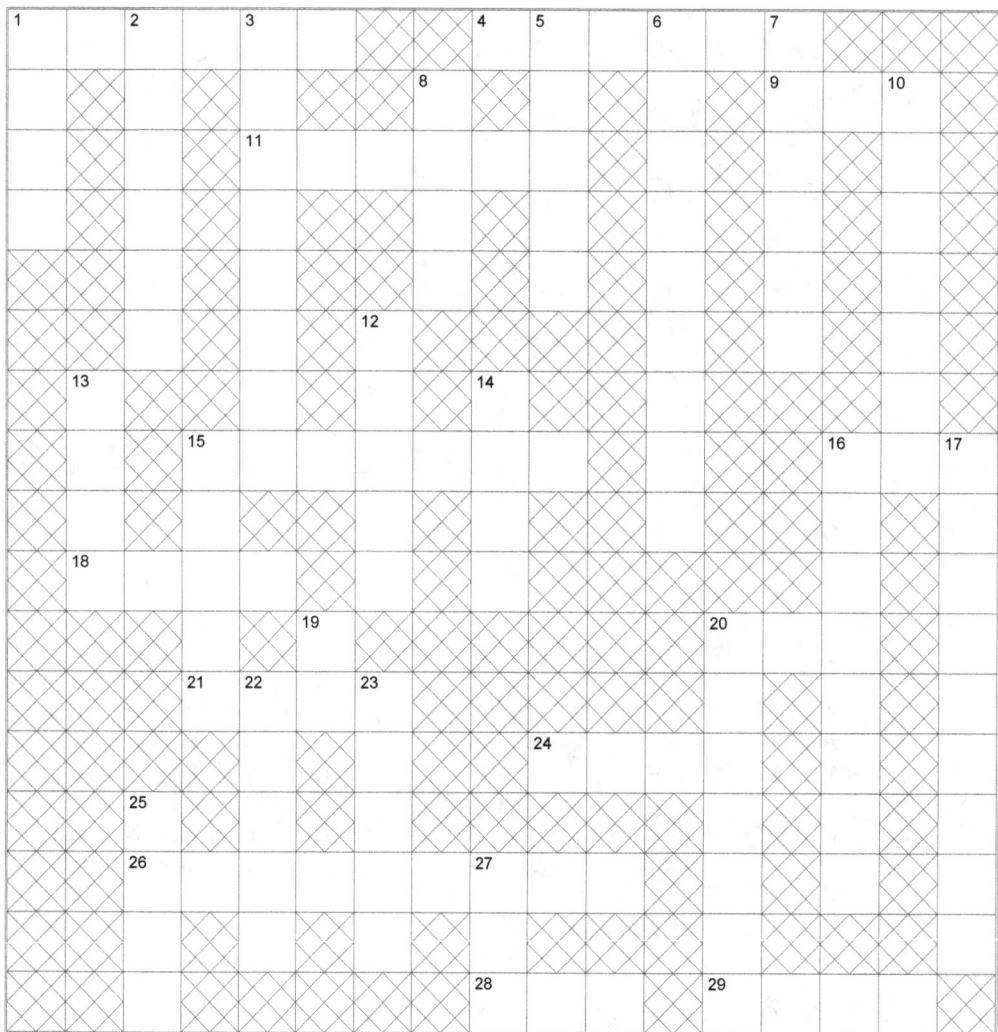

Across
1. Atticus's occupation
4. It plugged up the tree hole
9. Tom's left one had been cut off
11. Where Boo spent most of his time
15. Indian head ones were in the tree
16. Dill's initials
18. Mr. Deas; He escorted Helen
20. Object of the Radley Games
21. Tom was --- trying to escape
24. To end the life of something
26. Atticus's sister
28. Object found in the tree
29. Jem pushed Scout into the Radley's ---

Down
1. Woman at Cal's church who made Scout feel unwelcome
2. Boy Cunningham
3. Material proof
5. Bob or Mayella
6. What one gets at school
7. The judge for Tom's trial
8. Cal rubbed Walter's nose in it
10. Name of the town and county
12. Scout, Jem or Atticus, for example
13. It housed Tom Robinson while he waited for a trial
14. Jem had to do it for Mrs. Dubose
15. Jem's got caught on the fence
16. Miss Fisher
17. Word to describe Miss Gates
19. -- Kill A Mockingbird
20. Place from which Scout watched the trial
22. Mrs. Robinson
23. Process by which innocence or guilt is determined
25. Atticus's brother
27. Atticus shot a mad one

To Kill A Mockingbird Crossword 4 Answer Key

	1 L	2 A	3 W	Y	E	R		4 C	5 E	M	6 E	N	7 T		
	U	A	V				8 D		W		D		9 A	R	10 M
	L	L	11 I	N	S	I	D	E			U		Y		A
	A	T	D				R		L		C		L		Y
		E	E				T		L		A		O		C
		R	N		12 F						T		R		O
	13 J				I		14 R				I				M
	A	15 P	E	N	N	I	E	S			O		16 C	17 B	
	I	A			C		A				N		A	H	
	18 L	I	N	K		H		D					R	Y	
		N			19 T						20 B	O	O	P	
		T		21 S	22 H	23 O	T				A		L	O	
				E		R		24 K	I	L	L		I	C	
		25 J		L		I					C		N	R	
		26 A	L	E	X	A	N	27 D	R	A	O		E	I	
		C		N		L		O			N			T	
		K						28 G	U	M	29 Y	A	R	D	

Across
1. Atticus's occupation
4. It plugged up the tree hole
9. Tom's left one had been cut off
11. Where Boo spent most of his time
15. Indian head ones were in the tree
16. Dill's initials
18. Mr. Deas; He escorted Helen
20. Object of the Radley Games
21. Tom was --- trying to escape
24. To end the life of something
26. Atticus's sister
28. Object found in the tree
29. Jem pushed Scout into the Radley's ---

Down
1. Woman at Cal's church who made Scout feel unwelcome
2. Boy Cunningham
3. Material proof
5. Bob or Mayella
6. What one gets at school
7. The judge for Tom's trial
8. Cal rubbed Walter's nose in it
10. Name of the town and county
12. Scout, Jem or Atticus, for example
13. It housed Tom Robinson while he waited for a trial
14. Jem had to do it for Mrs. Dubose
15. Jem's got caught on the fence
16. Miss Fisher
17. Word to describe Miss Gates
19. -- Kill A Mockingbird
20. Place from which Scout watched the trial
22. Mrs. Robinson
23. Process by which innocence or guilt is determined
25. Atticus's brother
27. Atticus shot a mad one

To Kill A Mockingbird

TRIAL	LEE	READ	JURY	HAM
HELEN	CHURCH	ATTICUS	MISSIONARY	SUMMER
RAYMOND	CRIED	FREE SPACE	MAYCOMB	DUBOSE
BALCONY	COURTROOM	SCOUT	HYPOCRITE	CECIL
LINK	DILL	INSIDE	NORMAL	COOTIES

To Kill A Mockingbird

ALEXANDRA	CUNNINGHAM	BRUISES	WALTER	PRIDE
ZEEBO	FIGURES	CAKES	KILL	JEM
KIDS	GAME	FREE SPACE	EVIDENCE	GUILTY
MOCKINGBIRD	JAIL	PREJUDICE	CAROLINE	FINCH
MAUDIE	TREE	MAYELLA	CEMENT	MOB

To Kill A Mockingbird

DILL	CBH	AZALEAS	DIRT	WALTER
BOO	KNIFE	HELEN	YARD	CUNNINGHAM
GUM	EVIDENCE	FREE SPACE	FINCH	FIRE
GILMER	EDUCATION	COMPANY	PRIDE	CEMENT
CRAWFORD	BRUISES	LULA	MAUDIE	READ

To Kill A Mockingbird

SCOUT	LAWYER	KILL	ZEEBO	JEM
PANTS	JAIL	JURY	AUTHOR	HYPOCRITE
ATTICUS	MOB	FREE SPACE	TAYLOR	LINK
COOTIES	INSIDE	CHURCH	BACKGROUND	GUILTY
CAROLINE	SUMMER	MAYCOMB	CALPURNIA	NORMAL

To Kill A Mockingbird

NORMAL	COURTROOM	TATE	SHOT	SUMMER
GILMER	GAME	LEE	CUNNINGHAM	JAIL
BALCONY	MAUDIE	FREE SPACE	PULITZER	ALEXANDRA
AZALEAS	READ	CRAWFORD	PANTS	TO
COMPANY	ZEEBO	BACKGROUND	SCHOOL	ARM

To Kill A Mockingbird

DUBOSE	CAKES	CBH	TAYLOR	MAYELLA
LULA	HYPOCRITE	YARD	CRIED	BRUISES
GUM	ESCAPE	FREE SPACE	RAYMOND	WALTER
PENNIES	CAROLINE	CALPURNIA	KILL	EVIDENCE
PRIDE	MOB	KIDS	MOCKINGBIRD	SCOUT

To Kill A Mockingbird

CECIL	WALTER	CRAWFORD	ALEXANDRA	BALCONY
READ	CALPURNIA	SHOT	AZALEAS	MAYELLA
PREJUDICE	TATE	FREE SPACE	PULITZER	NORMAL
DIRT	EVIDENCE	BOO	SUMMER	GUM
MOB	MAUDIE	CAKES	DUBOSE	LULA

To Kill A Mockingbird

SYKES	LEE	CBH	YARD	CEMENT
FIRE	MOCKINGBIRD	RAYMOND	GILMER	CAROLINE
CRIED	KILL	FREE SPACE	COMPANY	GAME
JURY	PANTS	TREE	SCOUT	TAYLOR
EWELL	KIDS	HAM	CUNNINGHAM	COOTIES

To Kill A Mockingbird

FIRE	MAYELLA	TAYLOR	YARD	BOO
PANTS	MAYCOMB	JEM	DIRT	CEMENT
PENNIES	TRIAL	FREE SPACE	AUTHOR	ARM
LEE	MOB	EVIDENCE	ATTICUS	MOCKINGBIRD
AZALEAS	KIDS	TATE	ESCAPE	TO

To Kill A Mockingbird

NORMAL	READ	LAWYER	EWELL	GUILTY
RAYMOND	BRUISES	BACKGROUND	CUNNINGHAM	MAUDIE
JAIL	SCHOOL	FREE SPACE	DILL	CAROLINE
ALEXANDRA	SYKES	JURY	COMPANY	PAGEANT
CALPURNIA	COOTIES	GAME	ROBINSON	HELEN

To Kill A Mockingbird

EDUCATION	SUMMER	YARD	FIRE	JACK
RAYMOND	WALTER	TAYLOR	BRUISES	DILL
PRIDE	MAYCOMB	FREE SPACE	HYPOCRITE	CRIED
TATE	SCOUT	EVIDENCE	CECIL	LAWYER
CALPURNIA	CEMENT	READ	BRAVERY	MISSIONARY

To Kill A Mockingbird

GUILTY	TO	KIDS	CHURCH	COURTROOM
SHOT	MAUDIE	CAROLINE	COMPANY	CBH
PAGEANT	NORMAL	FREE SPACE	DOG	PANTS
MOB	AUTHOR	PENNIES	TREE	PULITZER
COOTIES	AZALEAS	LINK	ARM	MAYELLA

To Kill A Mockingbird

DUBOSE	EDUCATION	PULITZER	LEE	ZEEBO
LULA	JEM	SYKES	COOTIES	SCOUT
RAYMOND	ATTICUS	FREE SPACE	SUMMER	GUILTY
GUM	GAME	TO	YARD	MISSIONARY
ARM	CBH	WALTER	INSIDE	CHURCH

To Kill A Mockingbird

DOG	ALEXANDRA	TATE	CAKES	EWELL
AUTHOR	TAYLOR	CEMENT	DILL	CAROLINE
ESCAPE	SHOT	FREE SPACE	COMPANY	DIRT
MAYELLA	JURY	CUNNINGHAM	TREE	BRUISES
EVIDENCE	KILL	READ	BALCONY	AZALEAS

To Kill A Mockingbird

DUBOSE	GAME	EVIDENCE	CEMENT	CUNNINGHAM
ATTICUS	BOO	YARD	KILL	TO
GILMER	HYPOCRITE	FREE SPACE	PAGEANT	JURY
CRAWFORD	BALCONY	PANTS	JEM	JACK
ALEXANDRA	PENNIES	PRIDE	TATE	COMPANY

To Kill A Mockingbird

PREJUDICE	LINK	SUMMER	COURTROOM	ESCAPE
FIGURES	MAYCOMB	CAROLINE	DIRT	EDUCATION
INSIDE	CALPURNIA	FREE SPACE	CHURCH	MISSIONARY
WALTER	TAYLOR	READ	SYKES	MOCKINGBIRD
SCOUT	GUM	SCHOOL	BRUISES	ARM

To Kill A Mockingbird

KIDS	EWELL	BOO	PANTS	SCHOOL
CECIL	BALCONY	GILMER	SHOT	MOCKINGBIRD
LEE	READ	FREE SPACE	AUTHOR	CAKES
LINK	PENNIES	PREJUDICE	ALEXANDRA	CAROLINE
KILL	CALPURNIA	NORMAL	RAYMOND	MAYCOMB

To Kill A Mockingbird

INSIDE	GUM	PULITZER	DOG	BRAVERY
SYKES	TO	COMPANY	MISSIONARY	ATTICUS
GAME	KNIFE	FREE SPACE	TREE	TATE
GUILTY	MAUDIE	FINCH	LAWYER	CBH
DUBOSE	HELEN	DILL	BRUISES	JACK

To Kill A Mockingbird

MAUDIE	CUNNINGHAM	JACK	MOCKINGBIRD	PREJUDICE
EWELL	NORMAL	HAM	MISSIONARY	RAYMOND
LEE	LINK	FREE SPACE	GUILTY	CAKES
ZEEBO	EVIDENCE	EDUCATION	MAYCOMB	ROBINSON
INSIDE	GUM	BRUISES	HELEN	PANTS

To Kill A Mockingbird

DIRT	ALEXANDRA	TRIAL	FINCH	COMPANY
READ	BOO	LULA	DOG	JEM
TATE	CAROLINE	FREE SPACE	BALCONY	SYKES
PULITZER	PENNIES	GILMER	AUTHOR	BACKGROUND
KNIFE	JAIL	PAGEANT	SCOUT	MOB

To Kill A Mockingbird

HAM	SCOUT	CAROLINE	SYKES	GUM
YARD	CALPURNIA	CHURCH	GUILTY	PANTS
BRUISES	PENNIES	FREE SPACE	PREJUDICE	ATTICUS
FIGURES	BRAVERY	ARM	MISSIONARY	CRIED
DIRT	SUMMER	ZEEBO	SCHOOL	JACK

To Kill A Mockingbird

JEM	EWELL	MAUDIE	COOTIES	DILL
RAYMOND	COMPANY	FIRE	LAWYER	JAIL
HELEN	LEE	FREE SPACE	AUTHOR	MOCKINGBIRD
BALCONY	MAYELLA	PAGEANT	CBH	HYPOCRITE
LULA	DOG	DUBOSE	INSIDE	EDUCATION

To Kill A Mockingbird

GAME	SCHOOL	GUILTY	BRUISES	CAKES
NORMAL	SCOUT	EDUCATION	RAYMOND	TATE
DOG	MISSIONARY	FREE SPACE	FIGURES	GUM
GILMER	CBH	KILL	SHOT	CAROLINE
AUTHOR	JAIL	LINK	DILL	SYKES

To Kill A Mockingbird

TAYLOR	CRAWFORD	PENNIES	CHURCH	KNIFE
COURTROOM	HELEN	BACKGROUND	PRIDE	LAWYER
EWELL	DUBOSE	FREE SPACE	ZEEBO	READ
SUMMER	HYPOCRITE	CUNNINGHAM	ALEXANDRA	ROBINSON
CECIL	COOTIES	JURY	PAGEANT	ARM

To Kill A Mockingbird

BRAVERY	COMPANY	ROBINSON	BOO	DIRT
PULITZER	CHURCH	MISSIONARY	SHOT	JACK
COURTROOM	CRAWFORD	FREE SPACE	TO	CEMENT
NORMAL	KNIFE	SUMMER	DOG	BRUISES
EWELL	LULA	PREJUDICE	MAUDIE	RAYMOND

To Kill A Mockingbird

GUILTY	KIDS	GAME	BALCONY	SCHOOL
BACKGROUND	CAKES	ATTICUS	MAYELLA	TAYLOR
ESCAPE	GUM	FREE SPACE	HAM	TREE
KILL	HYPOCRITE	LINK	CUNNINGHAM	TRIAL
MAYCOMB	ZEEBO	JEM	AUTHOR	COOTIES

To Kill A Mockingbird

FIRE	DIRT	CBH	PAGEANT	JEM
MISSIONARY	GUILTY	PREJUDICE	READ	INSIDE
LINK	TRIAL	FREE SPACE	FIGURES	PENNIES
COURTROOM	LULA	EDUCATION	TAYLOR	ATTICUS
KILL	FINCH	HELEN	COOTIES	CECIL

To Kill A Mockingbird

TO	CUNNINGHAM	ESCAPE	GAME	CEMENT
GILMER	TREE	PRIDE	MAYELLA	MAYCOMB
JACK	BRAVERY	FREE SPACE	MAUDIE	AZALEAS
MOCKINGBIRD	MOB	BRUISES	LEE	GUM
CAROLINE	BOO	CAKES	LAWYER	KIDS

To Kill A Mockingbird

ARM	CAROLINE	TREE	SCOUT	FIGURES
FIRE	JACK	COURTROOM	CEMENT	INSIDE
JURY	LINK	FREE SPACE	HELEN	PENNIES
DIRT	EDUCATION	READ	TRIAL	YARD
CBH	RAYMOND	BACKGROUND	HAM	DUBOSE

To Kill A Mockingbird

CHURCH	TATE	CUNNINGHAM	KIDS	CRAWFORD
PANTS	MAYELLA	DILL	GUILTY	PREJUDICE
CALPURNIA	EWELL	FREE SPACE	GUM	AUTHOR
JAIL	SUMMER	JEM	BRUISES	LULA
ESCAPE	MAYCOMB	DOG	BRAVERY	SYKES

To Kill A Mockingbird

MAYCOMB	HAM	TO	PENNIES	DILL
CHURCH	LINK	ESCAPE	PREJUDICE	JEM
MOB	EVIDENCE	FREE SPACE	ATTICUS	JACK
ROBINSON	TREE	KILL	READ	SHOT
TATE	PULITZER	LAWYER	LEE	KIDS

To Kill A Mockingbird

HYPOCRITE	CUNNINGHAM	DOG	NORMAL	RAYMOND
BOO	SCHOOL	SCOUT	TAYLOR	CAROLINE
FINCH	CBH	FREE SPACE	BRAVERY	SUMMER
BALCONY	ARM	EDUCATION	FIGURES	COOTIES
HELEN	MOCKINGBIRD	YARD	CRAWFORD	FIRE

To Kill A Mockingbird Vocabulary Word List

No.	Word	Clue/Definition
1.	ACQUAINTED	Made familiar with
2.	ACQUIESCENCE	Passive agreement
3.	ACQUIRED	Obtained
4.	ADJACENT	Close to; next to
5.	ALLEGEDLY	Supposedly; believed to be so but not yet proved to be so
6.	AMIABLY	Good-naturedly; cordially
7.	ANTAGONIZE	Incur the dislike of someone; counteract
8.	APPREHENSION	Fearful feeling; dread
9.	ASCERTAINING	Finding out
10.	ASSESSMENT	Evaluation
11.	BEGRUDGE	To envy the possession or enjoyment of something
12.	CANTANKEROUS	Contrary; disagreeable; quarrelsome
13.	CHAMELEON	Changeable; like the lizard known for changing colors to blend in with its surroundings
14.	COMPENSATION	Something given or received as substitution or payment
15.	COMPLACENTLY	In a self-satisfied manner
16.	COMPROMISE	Settlement of differences in which concessions are made
17.	CONDESCENDED	Bring one's self down to an inferior level
18.	CONSENTED	Agreed to
19.	CONTEMPORARIES	Of or about the same age
20.	CONTRADICT	To go against
21.	DEBATING	Deliberating; considering
22.	DEFENDANT	Person against whom an action is brought
23.	DESOLATE	Deserted
24.	DISPELLED	To have done away with
25.	ECCENTRIC	Departing from the established norm, model or rule
26.	ECCLESIASTICAL	Pertaining to church
27.	ENCUMBERED	Hindered
28.	ENTRUSTED	Given over to another for care or protection
29.	EVASION	Act of avoiding
30.	EXTRACT	To forcibly draw forth; pull out
31.	FANATICAL	Possessed or driven by excessive zeal
32.	FRAUD	Deliberate deception for unfair or unlawful gain
33.	HYPOCRITES	People who say they believe one thing but actually believe in the opposite
34.	IMPROBABLE	Not likely
35.	INAUDIBLE	Unable to be heard
36.	INCONSPICUOUS	Not readily noticeable
37.	INCONVENIENCES	Things that cause trouble, lack of ease, or difficulty
38.	INDIGENOUS	Native
39.	INDULGE	To allow one a special pleasure
40.	INEVITABLE	Unavoidable; bound to happen
41.	INFALLIBLE	Unfailing; always correct
42.	INGENUOUS	Without sophistication; artless; innocent
43.	INTIMIDATION	Threats
44.	IRKED	Annoyed; bothered
45.	IRRELEVANT	not applicable; having nothing to do with the matter at hand
46.	ISOLATE	To separate from the group; set apart
47.	MALEVOLENT	Having ill-will; malicious
48.	MALIGNANT	Actively evil in nature
49.	MEDITATIVE	Thoughtful; reflective

To Kill A Mockingbird Vocabulary Word List

No.	Word	Clue/Definition
50.	OBLIVIOUS	Unaware
51.	OBSCURE	Inconspicuous; undistinguished; not well-known
52.	PAUPER	Poor person
53.	PENSIVE	Thoughtful
54.	PERIL	Danger
55.	PERPLEXITY	The condition of being puzzled
56.	PERSECUTED	Oppressed; ill-treated and harassed
57.	PERSEVERE	Remain constant to a purpose in spite of obstacles
58.	PREDICAMENT	Troublesome situation
59.	PREJUDICE	Preconceived preference or idea; bias
60.	PREOCCUPATION	The absorption of the attention or intellect
61.	PRONOUNCEMENTS	Authoritative statements
62.	PURSUITS	Activities; hobbies
63.	QUIBBLING	Making petty distinctions or irrelevant observations
64.	STEALTHY	Characterized by secret movement; avoiding notice
65.	SUBSEQUENT	Coming after
66.	SUBTLETY	Something not obvious
67.	SUSTAIN	To keep in existence; maintain; prolong
68.	TEETERED	Swayed back and forth unsteadily in a seesaw motion
69.	TORMENTING	Harassing; bothering; pestering
70.	TYRANNY	Extreme harshness; rigor
71.	UNANIMOUS	In complete agreement

Mockingbird Vocabulary Fill In The Blank 1

_____ 1. Finding out

_____ 2. Harassing; bothering; pestering

_____ 3. Characterized by secret movement; avoiding notice

_____ 4. Supposedly; believed to be so but not yet proved to be so

_____ 5. To separate from the group; set apart

_____ 6. Coming after

_____ 7. To go against

_____ 8. Agreed to

_____ 9. Act of avoiding

_____ 10. Oppressed; ill-treated and harassed

_____ 11. Contrary; disagreeable; quarrelsome

_____ 12. To forcibly draw forth; pull out

_____ 13. Unavoidable; bound to happen

_____ 14. To allow one a special pleasure

_____ 15. Annoyed; bothered

_____ 16. Passive agreement

_____ 17. To have done away with

_____ 18. In complete agreement

_____ 19. Unfailing; always correct

_____ 20. Thoughtful; reflective

Mockingbird Vocabulary Fill In The Blank 1 Answer Key

ASCERTAINING	1. Finding out
TORMENTING	2. Harassing; bothering; pestering
STEALTHY	3. Characterized by secret movement; avoiding notice
ALLEGEDLY	4. Supposedly; believed to be so but not yet proved to be so
ISOLATE	5. To separate from the group; set apart
SUBSEQUENT	6. Coming after
CONTRADICT	7. To go against
CONSENTED	8. Agreed to
EVASION	9. Act of avoiding
PERSECUTED	10. Oppressed; ill-treated and harassed
CANTANKEROUS	11. Contrary; disagreeable; quarrelsome
EXTRACT	12. To forcibly draw forth; pull out
INEVITABLE	13. Unavoidable; bound to happen
INDULGE	14. To allow one a special pleasure
IRKED	15. Annoyed; bothered
ACQUIESCENCE	16. Passive agreement
DISPELLED	17. To have done away with
UNANIMOUS	18. In complete agreement
INFALLIBLE	19. Unfailing; always correct
MEDITATIVE	20. Thoughtful; reflective

Mockingbird Vocabulary Fill In The Blank 2

1. Without sophistication; artless; innocent
2. Made familiar with
3. Bring one's self down to an inferior level
4. Actively evil in nature
5. Deliberating; considering
6. To keep in existence; maintain; prolong
7. Close to; next to
8. Unaware
9. Good-naturedly; cordially
10. Given over to another for care or protection
11. Inconspicuous; undistinguished; not well-known
12. Changeable; like the lizard known for changing colors to blend in with its surroundings
13. Troublesome situation
14. Activities; hobbies
15. The condition of being puzzled
16. Native
17. Hindered
18. not applicable; having nothing to do with the matter at hand
19. Extreme harshness; rigor
20. Danger

Mockingbird Vocabulary Fill In The Blank 2 Answer Key

INGENUOUS	1. Without sophistication; artless; innocent
ACQUAINTED	2. Made familiar with
CONDESCENDED	3. Bring one's self down to an inferior level
MALIGNANT	4. Actively evil in nature
DEBATING	5. Deliberating; considering
SUSTAIN	6. To keep in existence; maintain; prolong
ADJACENT	7. Close to; next to
OBLIVIOUS	8. Unaware
AMIABLY	9. Good-naturedly; cordially
ENTRUSTED	10. Given over to another for care or protection
OBSCURE	11. Inconspicuous; undistinguished; not well-known
CHAMELEON	12. Changeable; like the lizard known for changing colors to blend in with its surroundings
PREDICAMENT	13. Troublesome situation
PURSUITS	14. Activities; hobbies
PERPLEXITY	15. The condition of being puzzled
INDIGENOUS	16. Native
ENCUMBERED	17. Hindered
IRRELEVANT	18. not applicable; having nothing to do with the matter at hand
TYRANNY	19. Extreme harshness; rigor
PERIL	20. Danger

Mockingbird Vocabulary Fill In The Blank 3

1. The condition of being puzzled
2. Unaware
3. Inconspicuous; undistinguished; not well-known
4. Unfailing; always correct
5. Hindered
6. Pertaining to church
7. Not readily noticeable
8. The absorption of the attention or intellect
9. Deserted
10. Settlement of differences in which concessions are made
11. Of or about the same age
12. Incur the dislike of someone; counteract
13. To have done away with
14. Threats
15. To go against
16. To forcibly draw forth; pull out
17. Something given or received as substitution or payment
18. Poor person
19. Something not obvious
20. Act of avoiding

Mockingbird Vocabulary Fill In The Blank 3 Answer Key

PERPLEXITY	1. The condition of being puzzled
OBLIVIOUS	2. Unaware
OBSCURE	3. Inconspicuous; undistinguished; not well-known
INFALLIBLE	4. Unfailing; always correct
ENCUMBERED	5. Hindered
ECCLESIASTICAL	6. Pertaining to church
INCONSPICUOUS	7. Not readily noticeable
PREOCCUPATION	8. The absorption of the attention or intellect
DESOLATE	9. Deserted
COMPROMISE	10. Settlement of differences in which concessions are made
CONTEMPORARIES	11. Of or about the same age
ANTAGONIZE	12. Incur the dislike of someone; counteract
DISPELLED	13. To have done away with
INTIMIDATION	14. Threats
CONTRADICT	15. To go against
EXTRACT	16. To forcibly draw forth; pull out
COMPENSATION	17. Something given or received as substitution or payment
PAUPER	18. Poor person
SUBTLETY	19. Something not obvious
EVASION	20. Act of avoiding

Mockingbird Vocabulary Fill In The Blank 4

_____ 1. Evaluation

_____ 2. Harassing; bothering; pestering

_____ 3. not applicable; having nothing to do with the matter at hand

_____ 4. Actively evil in nature

_____ 5. Unaware

_____ 6. Thoughtful; reflective

_____ 7. Coming after

_____ 8. To allow one a special pleasure

_____ 9. Changeable; like the lizard known for changing colors to blend in with its surroundings

_____ 10. Act of avoiding

_____ 11. Remain constant to a purpose in spite of obstacles

_____ 12. Good-naturedly; cordially

_____ 13. Thoughtful

_____ 14. Close to; next to

_____ 15. Settlement of differences in which concessions are made

_____ 16. Poor person

_____ 17. Finding out

_____ 18. Hindered

_____ 19. To keep in existence; maintain; prolong

_____ 20. Authoritative statements

Mockingbird Vocabulary Fill In The Blank 4 Answer Key

ASSESSMENT	1. Evaluation
TORMENTING	2. Harassing; bothering; pestering
IRRELEVANT	3. not applicable; having nothing to do with the matter at hand
MALIGNANT	4. Actively evil in nature
OBLIVIOUS	5. Unaware
MEDITATIVE	6. Thoughtful; reflective
SUBSEQUENT	7. Coming after
INDULGE	8. To allow one a special pleasure
CHAMELEON	9. Changeable; like the lizard known for changing colors to blend in with its surroundings
EVASION	10. Act of avoiding
PERSEVERE	11. Remain constant to a purpose in spite of obstacles
AMIABLY	12. Good-naturedly; cordially
PENSIVE	13. Thoughtful
ADJACENT	14. Close to; next to
COMPROMISE	15. Settlement of differences in which concessions are made
PAUPER	16. Poor person
ASCERTAINING	17. Finding out
ENCUMBERED	18. Hindered
SUSTAIN	19. To keep in existence; maintain; prolong
PRONOUNCEMENTS	20. Authoritative statements

Mockingbird Vocabulary Matching 1

___ 1. STEALTHY   A. To allow one a special pleasure
___ 2. INEVITABLE   B. Preconceived preference or idea; bias
___ 3. PREDICAMENT   C. To keep in existence; maintain; prolong
___ 4. CONTRADICT   D. Troublesome situation
___ 5. COMPROMISE   E. Good-naturedly; cordially
___ 6. EXTRACT   F. Pertaining to church
___ 7. PENSIVE   G. Thoughtful; reflective
___ 8. FANATICAL   H. Without sophistication; artless; innocent
___ 9. AMIABLY   I. Native
___10. PAUPER   J. Thoughtful
___11. OBLIVIOUS   K. To forcibly draw forth; pull out
___12. INCONVENIENCES   L. Unaware
___13. INDULGE   M. To go against
___14. COMPENSATION   N. Characterized by secret movement; avoiding notice
___15. ADJACENT   O. Oppressed; ill-treated and harassed
___16. ENTRUSTED   P. not applicable; having nothing to do with the matter at hand
___17. IRRELEVANT   Q. Settlement of differences in which concessions are made
___18. INDIGENOUS   R. Person against whom an action is brought
___19. INGENUOUS   S. Possessed or driven by excessive zeal
___20. DEFENDANT   T. Given over to another for care or protection
___21. ECCLESIASTICAL   U. Close to; next to
___22. SUSTAIN   V. Something given or received as substitution or payment
___23. PREJUDICE   W. Unavoidable; bound to happen
___24. PERSECUTED   X. Poor person
___25. MEDITATIVE   Y. Things that cause trouble, lack of ease, or difficulty

Mockingbird Vocabulary Matching 1 Answer Key

N - 1. STEALTHY
W - 2. INEVITABLE
D - 3. PREDICAMENT
M - 4. CONTRADICT
Q - 5. COMPROMISE
K - 6. EXTRACT
J - 7. PENSIVE
S - 8. FANATICAL
E - 9. AMIABLY
X - 10. PAUPER
L - 11. OBLIVIOUS
Y - 12. INCONVENIENCES
A - 13. INDULGE
V - 14. COMPENSATION
U - 15. ADJACENT
T - 16. ENTRUSTED
P - 17. IRRELEVANT
I - 18. INDIGENOUS
H - 19. INGENUOUS
R - 20. DEFENDANT
F - 21. ECCLESIASTICAL
C - 22. SUSTAIN
B - 23. PREJUDICE
O - 24. PERSECUTED
G - 25. MEDITATIVE

A. To allow one a special pleasure
B. Preconceived preference or idea; bias
C. To keep in existence; maintain; prolong
D. Troublesome situation
E. Good-naturedly; cordially
F. Pertaining to church
G. Thoughtful; reflective
H. Without sophistication; artless; innocent
I. Native
J. Thoughtful
K. To forcibly draw forth; pull out
L. Unaware
M. To go against
N. Characterized by secret movement; avoiding notice
O. Oppressed; ill-treated and harassed
P. not applicable; having nothing to do with the matter at hand
Q. Settlement of differences in which concessions are made
R. Person against whom an action is brought
S. Possessed or driven by excessive zeal
T. Given over to another for care or protection
U. Close to; next to
V. Something given or received as substitution or payment
W. Unavoidable; bound to happen
X. Poor person
Y. Things that cause trouble, lack of ease, or difficulty

Mockingbird Vocabulary Matching 2

___ 1. IRKED A. Coming after
___ 2. DISPELLED B. Deliberate deception for unfair or unlawful gain
___ 3. INGENUOUS C. Passive agreement
___ 4. BEGRUDGE D. Good-naturedly; cordially
___ 5. FRAUD E. Obtained
___ 6. ENTRUSTED F. To envy the possession or enjoyment of something
___ 7. ECCENTRIC G. Swayed back and forth unsteadily in a seesaw motion
___ 8. OBSCURE H. Given over to another for care or protection
___ 9. SUBSEQUENT I. To have done away with
___10. CONDESCENDED J. Pertaining to church
___11. PREDICAMENT K. Deserted
___12. AMIABLY L. Things that cause trouble, lack of ease, or difficulty
___13. OBLIVIOUS M. Native
___14. COMPROMISE N. To keep in existence; maintain; prolong
___15. ACQUAINTED O. Settlement of differences in which concessions are made
___16. INCONVENIENCES P. Annoyed; bothered
___17. IRRELEVANT Q. Inconspicuous; undistinguished; not well-known
___18. INDIGENOUS R. Departing from the established norm, model or rule
___19. ECCLESIASTICAL S. not applicable; having nothing to do with the matter at hand
___20. ACQUIESCENCE T. Made familiar with
___21. HYPOCRITES U. Troublesome situation
___22. ACQUIRED V. Without sophistication; artless; innocent
___23. TEETERED W. Unaware
___24. DESOLATE X. People who say they believe one thing but actually believe in the opposite
___25. SUSTAIN Y. Bring one's self down to an inferior level

Mockingbird Vocabulary Matching 2 Answer Key

P - 1. IRKED		A. Coming after
I - 2. DISPELLED		B. Deliberate deception for unfair or unlawful gain
V - 3. INGENUOUS		C. Passive agreement
F - 4. BEGRUDGE		D. Good-naturedly; cordially
B - 5. FRAUD		E. Obtained
H - 6. ENTRUSTED		F. To envy the possession or enjoyment of something
R - 7. ECCENTRIC		G. Swayed back and forth unsteadily in a seesaw motion
Q - 8. OBSCURE		H. Given over to another for care or protection
A - 9. SUBSEQUENT		I. To have done away with
Y - 10. CONDESCENDED		J. Pertaining to church
U - 11. PREDICAMENT		K. Deserted
D - 12. AMIABLY		L. Things that cause trouble, lack of ease, or difficulty
W - 13. OBLIVIOUS		M. Native
O - 14. COMPROMISE		N. To keep in existence; maintain; prolong
T - 15. ACQUAINTED		O. Settlement of differences in which concessions are made
L - 16. INCONVENIENCES		P. Annoyed; bothered
S - 17. IRRELEVANT		Q. Inconspicuous; undistinguished; not well-known
M - 18. INDIGENOUS		R. Departing from the established norm, model or rule
J - 19. ECCLESIASTICAL		S. not applicable; having nothing to do with the matter at hand
C - 20. ACQUIESCENCE		T. Made familiar with
X - 21. HYPOCRITES		U. Troublesome situation
E - 22. ACQUIRED		V. Without sophistication; artless; innocent
G - 23. TEETERED		W. Unaware
K - 24. DESOLATE		X. People who say they believe one thing but actually believe in the opposite
N - 25. SUSTAIN		Y. Bring one's self down to an inferior level

Mockingbird Vocabulary Matching 3

___ 1. PURSUITS A. Good-naturedly; cordially
___ 2. FANATICAL B. Troublesome situation
___ 3. FRAUD C. The absorption of the attention or intellect
___ 4. CANTANKEROUS D. Incur the dislike of someone; counteract
___ 5. IRRELEVANT E. Act of avoiding
___ 6. DEFENDANT F. Swayed back and forth unsteadily in a seesaw motion
___ 7. TORMENTING G. Deliberate deception for unfair or unlawful gain
___ 8. PREOCCUPATION H. In complete agreement
___ 9. OBLIVIOUS I. Of or about the same age
___10. ECCENTRIC J. Activities; hobbies
___11. IMPROBABLE K. Making petty distinctions or irrelevant observations
___12. QUIBBLING L. Person against whom an action is brought
___13. AMIABLY M. Not readily noticeable
___14. INCONSPICUOUS N. Departing from the established norm, model or rule
___15. EVASION O. not applicable; having nothing to do with the matter at hand
___16. IRKED P. Unaware
___17. PERIL Q. Possessed or driven by excessive zeal
___18. UNANIMOUS R. Not likely
___19. MEDITATIVE S. Danger
___20. PREDICAMENT T. Thoughtful; reflective
___21. ANTAGONIZE U. Annoyed; bothered
___22. CONTEMPORARIES V. The condition of being puzzled
___23. ASCERTAINING W. Finding out
___24. TEETERED X. Harassing; bothering; pestering
___25. PERPLEXITY Y. Contrary; disagreeable; quarrelsome

Mockingbird Vocabulary Matching 3 Answer Key

J - 1. PURSUITS		A. Good-naturedly; cordially
Q - 2. FANATICAL		B. Troublesome situation
G - 3. FRAUD		C. The absorption of the attention or intellect
Y - 4. CANTANKEROUS		D. Incur the dislike of someone; counteract
O - 5. IRRELEVANT		E. Act of avoiding
L - 6. DEFENDANT		F. Swayed back and forth unsteadily in a seesaw motion
X - 7. TORMENTING		G. Deliberate deception for unfair or unlawful gain
C - 8. PREOCCUPATION		H. In complete agreement
P - 9. OBLIVIOUS		I. Of or about the same age
N - 10. ECCENTRIC		J. Activities; hobbies
R - 11. IMPROBABLE		K. Making petty distinctions or irrelevant observations
K - 12. QUIBBLING		L. Person against whom an action is brought
A - 13. AMIABLY		M. Not readily noticeable
M - 14. INCONSPICUOUS		N. Departing from the established norm, model or rule
E - 15. EVASION		O. not applicable; having nothing to do with the matter at hand
U - 16. IRKED		P. Unaware
S - 17. PERIL		Q. Possessed or driven by excessive zeal
H - 18. UNANIMOUS		R. Not likely
T - 19. MEDITATIVE		S. Danger
B - 20. PREDICAMENT		T. Thoughtful; reflective
D - 21. ANTAGONIZE		U. Annoyed; bothered
I - 22. CONTEMPORARIES		V. The condition of being puzzled
W - 23. ASCERTAINING		W. Finding out
F - 24. TEETERED		X. Harassing; bothering; pestering
V - 25. PERPLEXITY		Y. Contrary; disagreeable; quarrelsome

Mockingbird Vocabulary Matching 4

___ 1. ACQUIESCENCE   A. Authoritative statements
___ 2. EXTRACT   B. To separate from the group; set apart
___ 3. APPREHENSION   C. Making petty distinctions or irrelevant observations
___ 4. PREOCCUPATION   D. Passive agreement
___ 5. IRRELEVANT   E. To forcibly draw forth; pull out
___ 6. OBSCURE   F. Settlement of differences in which concessions are made
___ 7. ASSESSMENT   G. Swayed back and forth unsteadily in a seesaw motion
___ 8. OBLIVIOUS   H. Deliberating; considering
___ 9. ISOLATE   I. Evaluation
___ 10. COMPROMISE   J. Bring one's self down to an inferior level
___ 11. ANTAGONIZE   K. To have done away with
___ 12. DISPELLED   L. The absorption of the attention or intellect
___ 13. TEETERED   M. Departing from the established norm, model or rule
___ 14. QUIBBLING   N. Oppressed; ill-treated and harassed
___ 15. PRONOUNCEMENTS   O. People who say they believe one thing but actually believe in the opposite
___ 16. PERSEVERE   P. Native
___ 17. INDIGENOUS   Q. Remain constant to a purpose in spite of obstacles
___ 18. CONDESCENDED   R. Unaware
___ 19. ASCERTAINING   S. Given over to another for care or protection
___ 20. DEBATING   T. Without sophistication; artless; innocent
___ 21. HYPOCRITES   U. Fearful feeling; dread
___ 22. ENTRUSTED   V. Incur the dislike of someone; counteract
___ 23. PERSECUTED   W. not applicable; having nothing to do with the matter at hand
___ 24. INGENUOUS   X. Inconspicuous; undistinguished; not well-known
___ 25. ECCENTRIC   Y. Finding out

Mockingbird Vocabulary Matching 4 Answer Key

D - 1. ACQUIESCENCE	A.	Authoritative statements
E - 2. EXTRACT	B.	To separate from the group; set apart
U - 3. APPREHENSION	C.	Making petty distinctions or irrelevant observations
L - 4. PREOCCUPATION	D.	Passive agreement
W - 5. IRRELEVANT	E.	To forcibly draw forth; pull out
X - 6. OBSCURE	F.	Settlement of differences in which concessions are made
I - 7. ASSESSMENT	G.	Swayed back and forth unsteadily in a seesaw motion
R - 8. OBLIVIOUS	H.	Deliberating; considering
B - 9. ISOLATE	I.	Evaluation
F - 10. COMPROMISE	J.	Bring one's self down to an inferior level
V - 11. ANTAGONIZE	K.	To have done away with
K - 12. DISPELLED	L.	The absorption of the attention or intellect
G - 13. TEETERED	M.	Departing from the established norm, model or rule
C - 14. QUIBBLING	N.	Oppressed; ill-treated and harassed
A - 15. PRONOUNCEMENTS	O.	People who say they believe one thing but actually believe in the opposite
Q - 16. PERSEVERE	P.	Native
P - 17. INDIGENOUS	Q.	Remain constant to a purpose in spite of obstacles
J - 18. CONDESCENDED	R.	Unaware
Y - 19. ASCERTAINING	S.	Given over to another for care or protection
H - 20. DEBATING	T.	Without sophistication; artless; innocent
O - 21. HYPOCRITES	U.	Fearful feeling; dread
S - 22. ENTRUSTED	V.	Incur the dislike of someone; counteract
N - 23. PERSECUTED	W.	not applicable; having nothing to do with the matter at hand
T - 24. INGENUOUS	X.	Inconspicuous; undistinguished; not well-known
M - 25. ECCENTRIC	Y.	Finding out

Mockingbird Vocabulary Magic Squares 1

Match the definition with the vocabulary word. Put your answers in the magic squares below. When your answers are correct, all columns and rows will add to the same number.

A. ACQUIESCENCE
B. ASCERTAINING
C. BEGRUDGE
D. CONTEMPORARIES
E. MALIGNANT
F. APPREHENSION
G. INDULGE
H. ACQUAINTED
I. AMIABLY
J. PREDICAMENT
K. SUBSEQUENT
L. INCONVENIENCES
M. EVASION
N. ASSESSMENT
O. UNANIMOUS
P. INAUDIBLE

1. Made familiar with
2. Passive agreement
3. Finding out
4. To allow one a special pleasure
5. Troublesome situation
6. In complete agreement
7. Unable to be heard
8. Good-naturedly; cordially
9. Coming after
10. Evaluation
11. Act of avoiding
12. Things that cause trouble, lack of ease, or difficulty
13. Actively evil in nature
14. Of or about the same age
15. To envy the possession or enjoyment of something
16. Fearful feeling; dread

A=	B=	C=	D=
E=	F=	G=	H=
I=	J=	K=	L=
M=	N=	O=	P=

Mockingbird Vocabulary Magic Squares 1 Answer Key

Match the definition with the vocabulary word. Put your answers in the magic squares below. When your answers are correct, all columns and rows will add to the same number.

A. ACQUIESCENCE
B. ASCERTAINING
C. BEGRUDGE
D. CONTEMPORARIES
E. MALIGNANT
F. APPREHENSION
G. INDULGE
H. ACQUAINTED
I. AMIABLY
J. PREDICAMENT
K. SUBSEQUENT
L. INCONVENIENCES
M. EVASION
N. ASSESSMENT
O. UNANIMOUS
P. INAUDIBLE

1. Made familiar with
2. Passive agreement
3. Finding out
4. To allow one a special pleasure
5. Troublesome situation
6. In complete agreement
7. Unable to be heard
8. Good-naturedly; cordially
9. Coming after
10. Evaluation
11. Act of avoiding
12. Things that cause trouble, lack of ease, or difficulty
13. Actively evil in nature
14. Of or about the same age
15. To envy the possession or enjoyment of something
16. Fearful feeling; dread

A=2	B=3	C=15	D=14
E=13	F=16	G=4	H=1
I=8	J=5	K=9	L=12
M=11	N=10	O=6	P=7

Mockingbird Vocabulary Magic Squares 2

Match the definition with the vocabulary word. Put your answers in the magic squares below. When your answers are correct, all columns and rows will add to the same number.

A. PREDICAMENT
B. INCONSPICUOUS
C. CANTANKEROUS
D. ISOLATE
E. COMPENSATION
F. CONSENTED

G. IRKED
H. EVASION
I. DEFENDANT
J. CHAMELEON
K. INFALLIBLE
L. STEALTHY

M. INEVITABLE
N. INDULGE
O. PURSUITS
P. INDIGENOUS

1. Activities; hobbies
2. Changeable; like the lizard known for changing colors to blend in with its surroundings
3. Act of avoiding
4. Troublesome situation
5. To separate from the group; set apart
6. Something given or received as substitution or payment
7. Unfailing; always correct
8. To allow one a special pleasure
9. Agreed to
10. Contrary; disagreeable; quarrelsome
11. Unavoidable; bound to happen
12. Characterized by secret movement; avoiding notice
13. Person against whom an action is brought
14. Native
15. Not readily noticeable
16. Annoyed; bothered

A=	B=	C=	D=
E=	F=	G=	H=
I=	J=	K=	L=
M=	N=	O=	P=

Mockingbird Vocabulary Magic Squares 2 Answer Key

Match the definition with the vocabulary word. Put your answers in the magic squares below. When your answers are correct, all columns and rows will add to the same number.

A. PREDICAMENT
B. INCONSPICUOUS
C. CANTANKEROUS
D. ISOLATE
E. COMPENSATION
F. CONSENTED
G. IRKED
H. EVASION
I. DEFENDANT
J. CHAMELEON
K. INFALLIBLE
L. STEALTHY
M. INEVITABLE
N. INDULGE
O. PURSUITS
P. INDIGENOUS

1. Activities; hobbies
2. Changeable; like the lizard known for changing colors to blend in with its surroundings
3. Act of avoiding
4. Troublesome situation
5. To separate from the group; set apart
6. Something given or received as substitution or payment
7. Unfailing; always correct
8. To allow one a special pleasure
9. Agreed to
10. Contrary; disagreeable; quarrelsome
11. Unavoidable; bound to happen
12. Characterized by secret movement; avoiding notice
13. Person against whom an action is brought
14. Native
15. Not readily noticeable
16. Annoyed; bothered

A=4	B=15	C=10	D=5
E=6	F=9	G=16	H=3
I=13	J=2	K=7	L=12
M=11	N=8	O=1	P=14

Mockingbird Vocabulary Magic Squares 3

Match the definition with the vocabulary word. Put your answers in the magic squares below. When your answers are correct, all columns and rows will add to the same number.

A. TEETERED
B. PRONOUNCEMENTS
C. ACQUAINTED
D. SUSTAIN
E. PERIL
F. ANTAGONIZE
G. INTIMIDATION
H. TORMENTING
I. CONDESCENDED
J. EVASION
K. MEDITATIVE
L. DEFENDANT
M. CHAMELEON
N. PREDICAMENT
O. COMPROMISE
P. QUIBBLING

1. Incur the dislike of someone; counteract
2. Bring one's self down to an inferior level
3. Settlement of differences in which concessions are made
4. To keep in existence; maintain; prolong
5. Changeable; like the lizard known for changing colors to blend in with its surroundings
6. Authoritative statements
7. Harassing; bothering; pestering
8. Thoughtful; reflective
9. Made familiar with
10. Making petty distinctions or irrelevant observations
11. Act of avoiding
12. Danger
13. Person against whom an action is brought
14. Threats
15. Swayed back and forth unsteadily in a seesaw motion
16. Troublesome situation

A=	B=	C=	D=
E=	F=	G=	H=
I=	J=	K=	L=
M=	N=	O=	P=

Mockingbird Vocabulary Magic Squares 3 Answer Key

Match the definition with the vocabulary word. Put your answers in the magic squares below. When your answers are correct, all columns and rows will add to the same number.

A. TEETERED	G. INTIMIDATION	M. CHAMELEON
B. PRONOUNCEMENTS	H. TORMENTING	N. PREDICAMENT
C. ACQUAINTED	I. CONDESCENDED	O. COMPROMISE
D. SUSTAIN	J. EVASION	P. QUIBBLING
E. PERIL	K. MEDITATIVE	
F. ANTAGONIZE	L. DEFENDANT	

1. Incur the dislike of someone; counteract
2. Bring one's self down to an inferior level
3. Settlement of differences in which concessions are made
4. To keep in existence; maintain; prolong
5. Changeable; like the lizard known for changing colors to blend in with its surroundings
6. Authoritative statements
7. Harassing; bothering; pestering
8. Thoughtful; reflective
9. Made familiar with
10. Making petty distinctions or irrelevant observations
11. Act of avoiding
12. Danger
13. Person against whom an action is brought
14. Threats
15. Swayed back and forth unsteadily in a seesaw motion
16. Troublesome situation

A=15	B=6	C=9	D=4
E=12	F=1	G=14	H=7
I=2	J=11	K=8	L=13
M=5	N=16	O=3	P=10

Mockingbird Vocabulary Magic Squares 4

Match the definition with the vocabulary word. Put your answers in the magic squares below. When your answers are correct, all columns and rows will add to the same number.

A. ASSESSMENT
B. HYPOCRITES
C. IMPROBABLE
D. INAUDIBLE
E. PREDICAMENT
F. ENTRUSTED
G. PREOCCUPATION
H. DESOLATE
I. ALLEGEDLY
J. INTIMIDATION
K. PERPLEXITY
L. INDULGE
M. PENSIVE
N. EXTRACT
O. CONTRADICT
P. DEBATING

1. Thoughtful
2. Given over to another for care or protection
3. Deserted
4. To go against
5. To allow one a special pleasure
6. Not likely
7. Evaluation
8. Threats
9. The condition of being puzzled
10. Unable to be heard
11. People who say they believe one thing but actually believe in the opposite
12. Supposedly; believed to be so but not yet proved to be so
13. To forcibly draw forth; pull out
14. Troublesome situation
15. The absorption of the attention or intellect
16. Deliberating; considering

A=	B=	C=	D=
E=	F=	G=	H=
I=	J=	K=	L=
M=	N=	O=	P=

Mockingbird Vocabulary Magic Squares 4 Answer Key

Match the definition with the vocabulary word. Put your answers in the magic squares below. When your answers are correct, all columns and rows will add to the same number.

A. ASSESSMENT
B. HYPOCRITES
C. IMPROBABLE
D. INAUDIBLE
E. PREDICAMENT
F. ENTRUSTED
G. PREOCCUPATION
H. DESOLATE
I. ALLEGEDLY
J. INTIMIDATION
K. PERPLEXITY
L. INDULGE
M. PENSIVE
N. EXTRACT
O. CONTRADICT
P. DEBATING

1. Thoughtful
2. Given over to another for care or protection
3. Deserted
4. To go against
5. To allow one a special pleasure
6. Not likely
7. Evaluation
8. Threats
9. The condition of being puzzled
10. Unable to be heard
11. People who say they believe one thing but actually believe in the opposite
12. Supposedly; believed to be so but not yet proved to be so
13. To forcibly draw forth; pull out
14. Troublesome situation
15. The absorption of the attention or intellect
16. Deliberating; considering

A=7	B=11	C=6	D=10
E=14	F=2	G=15	H=3
I=12	J=8	K=9	L=5
M=1	N=13	O=4	P=16

Mockingbird Vocabulary Word Search 1

```
C A N T A N K E R O U S H K C V A A B K
Z W T P E G D U R G E B H R S C S D P T
T J N F E J T N A N G I L A M V S J A Y
X Z A W M R I N D I G E N O U S E A N W
X P D F N M S L Y T E L T B U S S C T D
C O N S E N T E D A K N P S K U S E A X
S T E A L T H Y V B Q P C C O P M N G Z
I N F A L L I B L E I N D U L G E T O W
P E E V L V M R N D R D N R M C N R N R
U T D C D Q P T L M E E Y E C B T D I P
R A C Q U I R E D K G D N E G P E E Z L
S L M X H U O S R N U O N M A E Y R E R
U O S I S Z B I I A I T Y U X N P E E C
I S X T A F A J R S R N P Q N S N T S D
T E E W C B B F A I M E Q A J I V E H G
S D M Q Y P L V C L R Q R S C V Q E C S
T C A R T X E Y C Y Z Y Q D X E F T Y K
I S O L A T E L B A T I V E N I Z X T F
```

Act of avoiding (7)
Actively evil in nature (9)
Activities; hobbies (8)
Agreed to (9)
Annoyed; bothered (5)
Characterized by secret movement; avoiding notice (8)
Close to; next to (8)
Contrary; disagreeable; quarrelsome (12)
Danger (5)
Deliberate deception for unfair or unlawful gain (5)
Deliberating; considering (8)
Departing from the established norm, model or rule (9)
Deserted (8)
Evaluation (10)
Extreme harshness; rigor (7)
Given over to another for care or protection (9)
Good-naturedly; cordially (7)
Hindered (10)
Inconspicuous; undistinguished; not well-known (7)
Incur the dislike of someone; counteract (10)
Native (10)
Not likely (10)
Obtained (8)
Person against whom an action is brought (9)
Poor person (6)
Remain constant to a purpose in spite of obstacles (9)
Something not obvious (8)
Swayed back and forth unsteadily in a seesaw motion (8)
Thoughtful (7)
To allow one a special pleasure (7)
To envy the possession or enjoyment of something (8)
To forcibly draw forth; pull out (7)
To separate from the group; set apart (7)
Unavoidable; bound to happen (10)
Unfailing; always correct (10)
Without sophistication; artless; innocent (9)

Mockingbird Vocabulary Word Search 1 Answer Key

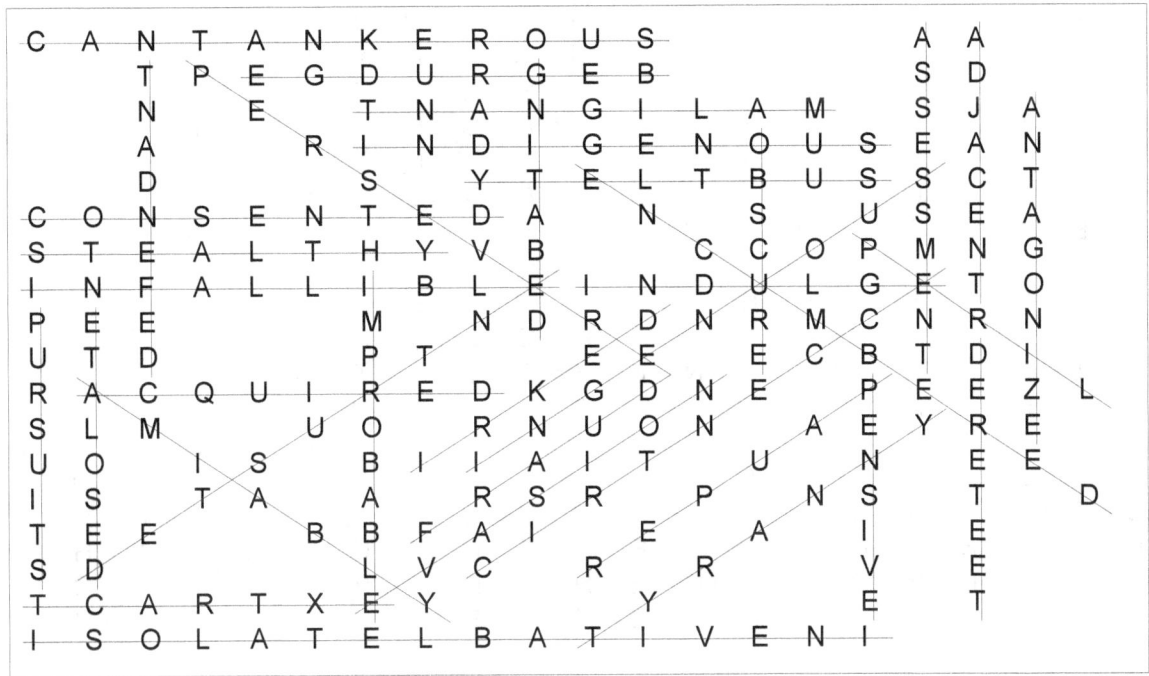

Act of avoiding (7)
Actively evil in nature (9)
Activities; hobbies (8)
Agreed to (9)
Annoyed; bothered (5)
Characterized by secret movement; avoiding notice (8)
Close to; next to (8)
Contrary; disagreeable; quarrelsome (12)
Danger (5)
Deliberate deception for unfair or unlawful gain (5)
Deliberating; considering (8)
Departing from the established norm, model or rule (9)
Deserted (8)
Evaluation (10)
Extreme harshness; rigor (7)
Given over to another for care or protection (9)
Good-naturedly; cordially (7)
Hindered (10)
Inconspicuous; undistinguished; not well-known (7)
Incur the dislike of someone; counteract (10)
Native (10)
Not likely (10)
Obtained (8)
Person against whom an action is brought (9)
Poor person (6)
Remain constant to a purpose in spite of obstacles (9)
Something not obvious (8)
Swayed back and forth unsteadily in a seesaw motion (8)
Thoughtful (7)
To allow one a special pleasure (7)
To envy the possession or enjoyment of something (8)
To forcibly draw forth; pull out (7)
To separate from the group; set apart (7)
Unavoidable; bound to happen (10)
Unfailing; always correct (10)
Without sophistication; artless; innocent (9)

Mockingbird Vocabulary Word Search 2

```
M E D I T A T I V E P U R S U I T S G B
S D K N V L S X N E N Y U U Q I C A H L
P P Z Z D O Z C N A G O O O Q N A P C C
W A H S L Q U S N C U G B I V C R P P G
L U N A K M I I G N L R S V P O T R E K
X P T C B V M E E C R I C I E N X E R H
B E T E E O N G V B N K U L Z S E H P K
K R R N U J N N L A J E R B I P T E L P
I E D S S I P A U C S S E O N I A N E J
D N L F U Q C D T K Q I F M O C L S X M
F N D Y B I I E C P L M O R G U O I I G
X H N U T B E Q O T E O J N A O S O T H
S T E A L T H Y N N A R Y T T U E N Y E
S Y N E E G H L T A D P I C N S D L G C
M A D R T C E B R D J M P L A N Q D C D
F K E B Y R Y A A N A O Y W Y M U T Z Q
C D K D S S R I D E C C E N T R I C K V
L K R B W K N M I F E Y C Y G T M F X H
S J I M V W Z A C E N H D E B A T I N G
A C Q U I R E D T D T V B S U S T A I N
```

Act of avoiding (7)
Activities; hobbies (8)
Annoyed; bothered (5)
Characterized by secret movement; avoiding notice (8)
Close to; next to (8)
Danger (5)
Deliberate deception for unfair or unlawful gain (5)
Deliberating; considering (8)
Departing from the established norm, model or rule (9)
Deserted (8)
Extreme harshness; rigor (7)
Fearful feeling; dread (12)
Good-naturedly; cordially (7)
Hindered (10)
In complete agreement (9)
Inconspicuous; undistinguished; not well-known (7)
Incur the dislike of someone; counteract (10)
Not readily noticeable (13)
Obtained (8)
Person against whom an action is brought (9)
Poor person (6)
Possessed or driven by excessive zeal (9)
Settlement of differences in which concessions are made (10)
Something not obvious (8)
Swayed back and forth unsteadily in a seesaw motion (8)
The condition of being puzzled (10)
Thoughtful (7)
Thoughtful; reflective (10)
To allow one a special pleasure (7)
To envy the possession or enjoyment of something (8)
To forcibly draw forth; pull out (7)
To go against (10)
To keep in existence; maintain; prolong (7)
To separate from the group; set apart (7)
Unable to be heard (9)
Unaware (9)
Without sophistication; artless; innocent (9)

Mockingbird Vocabulary Word Search 2 Answer Key

Act of avoiding (7)
Activities; hobbies (8)
Annoyed; bothered (5)
Characterized by secret movement; avoiding notice (8)
Close to; next to (8)
Danger (5)
Deliberate deception for unfair or unlawful gain (5)
Deliberating; considering (8)
Departing from the established norm, model or rule (9)
Deserted (8)
Extreme harshness; rigor (7)
Fearful feeling; dread (12)
Good-naturedly; cordially (7)
Hindered (10)
In complete agreement (9)
Inconspicuous; undistinguished; not well-known (7)
Incur the dislike of someone; counteract (10)
Not readily noticeable (13)
Obtained (8)

Person against whom an action is brought (9)
Poor person (6)
Possessed or driven by excessive zeal (9)
Settlement of differences in which concessions are made (10)
Something not obvious (8)
Swayed back and forth unsteadily in a seesaw motion (8)
The condition of being puzzled (10)
Thoughtful (7)
Thoughtful; reflective (10)
To allow one a special pleasure (7)
To envy the possession or enjoyment of something (8)
To forcibly draw forth; pull out (7)
To go against (10)
To keep in existence; maintain; prolong (7)
To separate from the group; set apart (7)
Unable to be heard (9)
Unaware (9)
Without sophistication; artless; innocent (9)

Mockingbird Vocabulary Word Search 3

```
I N F A L L I B L E Z I N O G A T N A D
N S J M E W J N C G L M C J G S O I D V
D C O B L D M C D D F Q J X Q I Z A E X
I P U L B M E T X U T C A R T X E T B D
G R N T A N N N S R L G Q A V I W S A L
E E A Y T T X J C G D G S A N O S U M
N O N R I L E Q V E P N E C J B Z S I S
O C I A V Z K B T B E Y O Q I S V S N S
U C M N E S M N D P W N P U M C P G M
S U O N N S E U M J S B S A P U C C C F
E P U Y I S A O T P M T B I R R O R O Z
T A S Q N R C M I E H S V N O E N T N A
I T L O F H Q C N D E W J T B C T H D K
R I C L N Q U Z A N N E T Y E A X R J E R
C O X L E O I N U W R S E D B S A E S F
O N P F U G R P D H E D O R L C D V E M
P E N S I V E D I S P E L L E D I A E P
Y Z B Y J R D D B F U K B N A D C S N D
H C R W I V P T L Y A R T F R T I D M
Y T E L T B U S E Y P I X J L G E O E X
P E R P L E X I T Y L B A I M A Z N D K
```

ACQUAINTED	DISPELLED	IRKED
ACQUIRED	ECCENTRIC	ISOLATE
ADJACENT	EVASION	OBSCURE
ALLEGEDLY	EXTRACT	PAUPER
AMIABLY	FRAUD	PENSIVE
ANTAGONIZE	HYPOCRITES	PERIL
BEGRUDGE	IMPROBABLE	PERPLEXITY
COMPENSATION	INAUDIBLE	PREOCCUPATION
CONDESCENDED	INCONSPICUOUS	SUBTLETY
CONSENTED	INDIGENOUS	SUSTAIN
CONTRADICT	INDULGE	TEETERED
DEBATING	INEVITABLE	TYRANNY
DESOLATE	INFALLIBLE	UNANIMOUS

Mockingbird Vocabulary Word Search 3 Answer Key

ACQUAINTED	DISPELLED	IRKED
ACQUIRED	ECCENTRIC	ISOLATE
ADJACENT	EVASION	OBSCURE
ALLEGEDLY	EXTRACT	PAUPER
AMIABLY	FRAUD	PENSIVE
ANTAGONIZE	HYPOCRITES	PERIL
BEGRUDGE	IMPROBABLE	PERPLEXITY
COMPENSATION	INAUDIBLE	PREOCCUPATION
CONDESCENDED	INCONSPICUOUS	SUBTLETY
CONSENTED	INDIGENOUS	SUSTAIN
CONTRADICT	INDULGE	TEETERED
DEBATING	INEVITABLE	TYRANNY
DESOLATE	INFALLIBLE	UNANIMOUS

Mockingbird Vocabulary Word Search 4

```
I N F A L L I B L E A M I A B L Y E A N W
N N C S F X C N W S C K X L P G S X T R J
D P D K U A O V E B Q G F W A V U T A M T
U E I I T B N P T V U C T S U T O R G R J
L R N H G L S A E K I V L P P R E C O M T
G P A Y X E E T R E T E Z E H Y K T N B G
E L U T X P N P Q I S N A Q R Y K T I G G
G E D E F Y T O Y U C E D B H Q N E Z D B
D X I L N N E D U U E A V T L O A E W M
U I B T Q T D F M S N N L E I E T T E B M
R T L B O L R B O B C A T T R Z N E W M
G Y E U D R E U C B E F A C P E A R P T
E D S S S R M I S T S P D O D L C E P Y
B E F Z E U R E S T U C J M T T C D R Y K
H R S D D T S T N C E G U P Y P Z E S K D
D I Y N N R Z T C T V D S R J L J S C D Y
J U W E T P S O A Z I T A O E U Q O U Y
X Q C S G E E Q V I S N N M D D V L U Y
T C I D A R T N O C N V G I S O L A T E D
E A P X P I R L G Y E J C S L Z R T E X C
I R K E D L K Q K K P E L E H F B E D C
```

ACQUIESCENCE
ACQUIRED
AMIABLY
ANTAGONIZE
BEGRUDGE
CANTANKEROUS
COMPROMISE
CONSENTED
CONTRADICT
DESOLATE
ECCENTRIC
ENCUMBERED
ENTRUSTED

EXTRACT
FANATICAL
FRAUD
INAUDIBLE
INDIGENOUS
INDULGE
INEVITABLE
INFALLIBLE
IRKED
ISOLATE
OBSCURE
PAUPER
PENSIVE

PERIL
PERPLEXITY
PERSECUTED
PERSEVERE
PREJUDICE
PREOCCUPATION
STEALTHY
SUBSEQUENT
SUBTLETY
SUSTAIN
TEETERED
TORMENTING
TYRANNY

Mockingbird Vocabulary Word Search 4 Answer Key

I	N	F	A	L	L	I	B	L	E	A	M	I	A	B	L	Y	E	A
N	N		S		F		C	N		C				P		S	X	N
D	P	D		U	A	O		E		Q				A		U	T	T
U	E	I	I		B	N	P		V	U				U		O	R	A
L	R	N		G		S	A	E		I				P		R	A	G
G	P	A	Y		E	E	T	R	E	T	E			E		E	C	O
E	L	U	T			N		Q		S	N	A		R	B	K	T	N
G	E	D				T			U		E	V	T		H	N	E	I
D	X	I	L	N		E	D	O	U	U	E	A	L	O	A	A	T	Z
U	I	B	T	T		D	M	S	N	C	L	T	E	T	T	E	E
R	T	L	B	O	R	B	O	C	A	T	R		E	N	R
G	Y	E	U	O	R	E	U	C	B	E	A	C		A	E			P
E	D		S	S	R	M	I	S	T	S	P	O		C	E			E
B	E		E	U	R	E	S	T	U	C		M	T		D			P
	R			D	T	S	N	C	E	D	U	P	Y		E	J		S
	I				N		T	C	T	V	D				S	O		E
	U				E	P		O	A	I	S	N	A		O	E	U	C
	Q	C				E	E		I	S	N		G	M	D		L	U
T	C	I	D	A	R	T	N	O	C	N	E		I	S	O	L	A	T	E
E	A			P	I			Y	E		C	S		R	T	E
I	R	K	E	D	L			P	E	E		F		E	D

ACQUIESCENCE	EXTRACT	PERIL
ACQUIRED	FANATICAL	PERPLEXITY
AMIABLY	FRAUD	PERSECUTED
ANTAGONIZE	INAUDIBLE	PERSEVERE
BEGRUDGE	INDIGENOUS	PREJUDICE
CANTANKEROUS	INDULGE	PREOCCUPATION
COMPROMISE	INEVITABLE	STEALTHY
CONSENTED	INFALLIBLE	SUBSEQUENT
CONTRADICT	IRKED	SUBTLETY
DESOLATE	ISOLATE	SUSTAIN
ECCENTRIC	OBSCURE	TEETERED
ENCUMBERED	PAUPER	TORMENTING
ENTRUSTED	PENSIVE	TYRANNY

Mockingbird Vocabulary Crossword 1

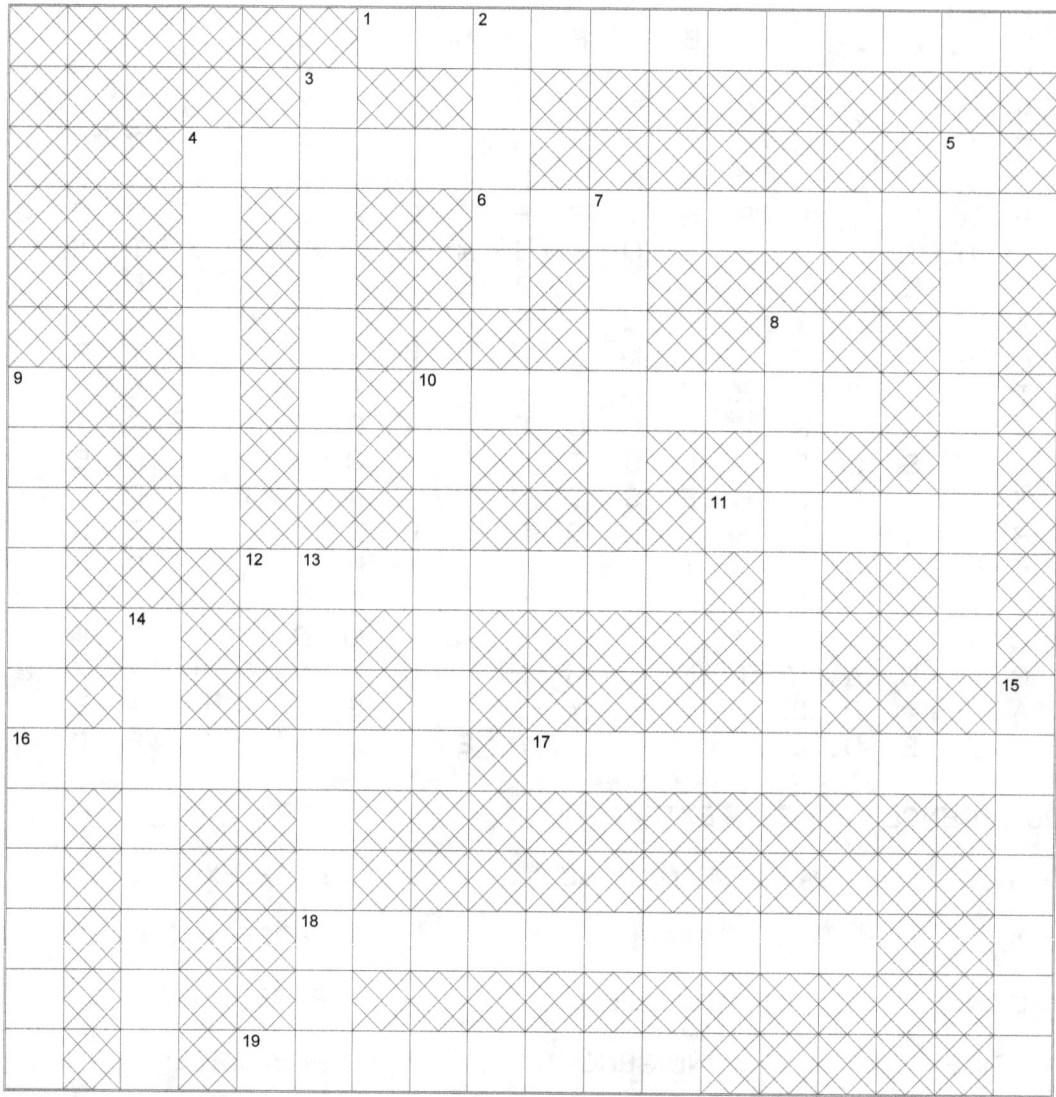

Across
1. Fearful feeling; dread
4. Poor person
6. Unfailing; always correct
10. Obtained
11. Annoyed; bothered
12. Close to; next to
16. Something not obvious
17. Changeable; like the lizard known for changing colors to blend in with its surroundings
18. Made familiar with
19. Characterized by secret movement; avoiding notice

Down
2. Danger
3. To keep in existence; maintain; prolong
4. Thoughtful
5. Supposedly; believed to be so but not yet proved to be so
7. Deliberate deception for unfair or unlawful gain
8. To envy the possession or enjoyment of something
9. Passive agreement
10. Good-naturedly; cordially
13. Person against whom an action is brought
14. Deliberating; considering
15. To allow one a special pleasure

Mockingbird Vocabulary Crossword 1 Answer Key

Across
1. Fearful feeling; dread
4. Poor person
6. Unfailing; always correct
10. Obtained
11. Annoyed; bothered
12. Close to; next to
16. Something not obvious
17. Changeable; like the lizard known for changing colors to blend in with its surroundings
18. Made familiar with
19. Characterized by secret movement; avoiding notice

Down
2. Danger
3. To keep in existence; maintain; prolong
4. Thoughtful
5. Supposedly; believed to be so but not yet proved to be so
7. Deliberate deception for unfair or unlawful gain
8. To envy the possession or enjoyment of something
9. Passive agreement
10. Good-naturedly; cordially
13. Person against whom an action is brought
14. Deliberating; considering
15. To allow one a special pleasure

Mockingbird Vocabulary Crossword 2

Across
5. Things that cause trouble, lack of ease, or difficulty
10. Poor person
11. Danger
13. Annoyed; bothered
16. To separate from the group; set apart
17. Characterized by secret movement; avoiding notice
18. Deliberate deception for unfair or unlawful gain
19. In complete agreement
20. Thoughtful

Down
1. Inconspicuous; undistinguished; not well-known
2. Given over to another for care or protection
3. Swayed back and forth unsteadily in a seesaw motion
4. Obtained
5. Unfailing; always correct
6. Settlement of differences in which concessions are made
7. Hindered
8. Something not obvious
9. Fearful feeling; dread
12. Not likely
13. Without sophistication; artless; innocent
14. To keep in existence; maintain; prolong
15. Extreme harshness; rigor

Mockingbird Vocabulary Crossword 2 Answer Key

		1 O				2 E		3 T			4 A	
		B	5 I	6 C	O	N	V	E	N	7 I	E	N	C	8 S
		S	N	O		T		E		N	Q	U
9 A	C	F		R		E		T		C	U	B
P	U	A	10 P	A	U	P	E	R		U	I	T
11 P	E	R	I	L	R		S	R		M	R	L
R	E	L		O	T		E	E		B	E	E
E		I		M	E		D			E	D	T
H	12 I	B		I	D					R		Y
E	M	L		S		13 I	R	K	E	D		
N	P	E	14 S	E		N			D			
S	R		U			G				15 T		
16 I	S	O	L	A	T	E	17 S	T	E	A	L	T	H	Y
O	B						T			N		R
N	A						A			U	18 F	R	A	U	D
	B		19 U	N	A	N	I	M	O	U	S		N
	L						N			U		N
	20 P	E	N	S	I	V	E			S		Y

Across
5. Things that cause trouble, lack of ease, or difficulty
10. Poor person
11. Danger
13. Annoyed; bothered
16. To separate from the group; set apart
17. Characterized by secret movement; avoiding notice
18. Deliberate deception for unfair or unlawful gain
19. In complete agreement
20. Thoughtful

Down
1. Inconspicuous; undistinguished; not well-known
2. Given over to another for care or protection
3. Swayed back and forth unsteadily in a seesaw motion
4. Obtained
5. Unfailing; always correct
6. Settlement of differences in which concessions are made
7. Hindered
8. Something not obvious
9. Fearful feeling; dread
12. Not likely
13. Without sophistication; artless; innocent
14. To keep in existence; maintain; prolong
15. Extreme harshness; rigor

Mockingbird Vocabulary Crossword 3

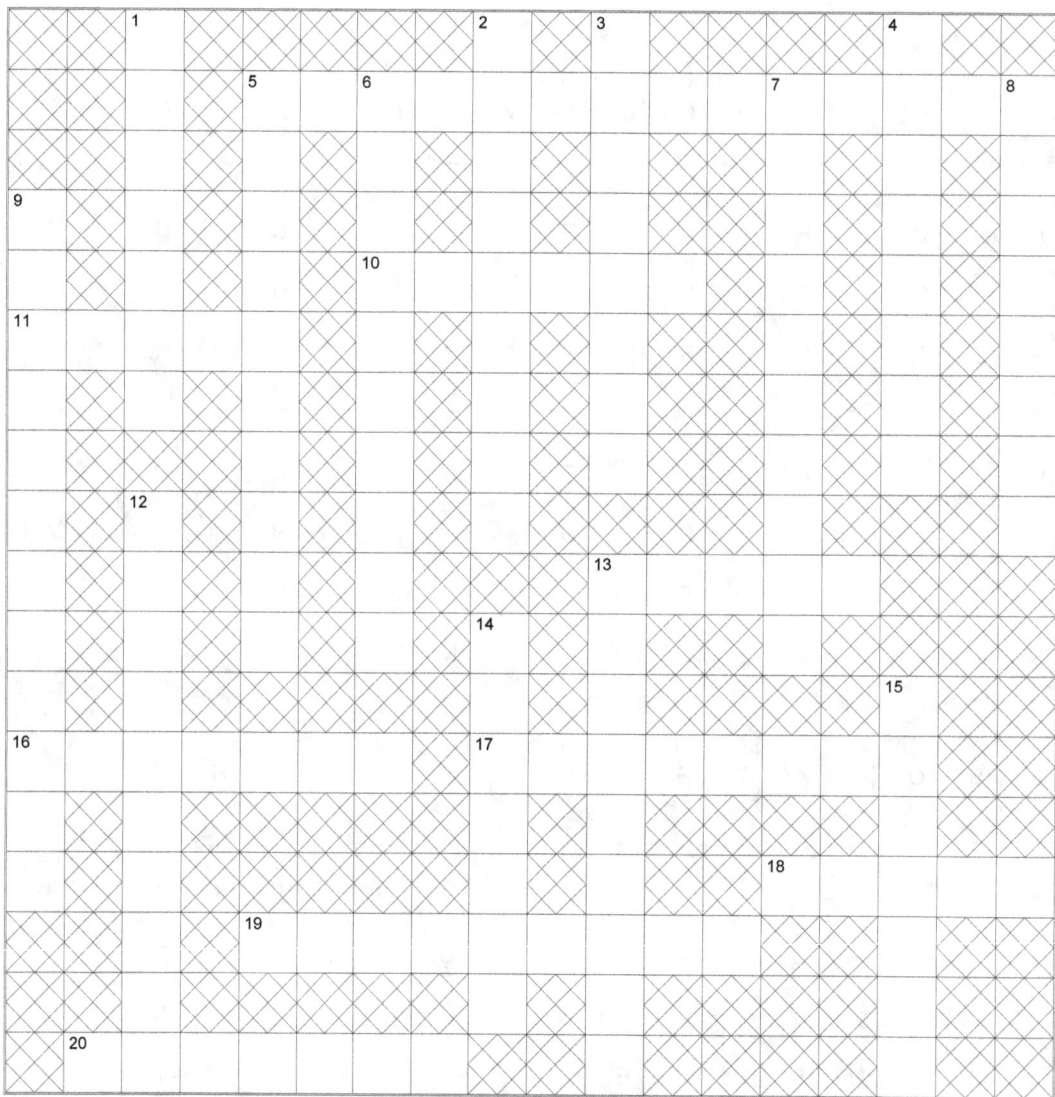

Across
5. Things that cause trouble, lack of ease, or difficulty
10. Poor person
11. Danger
13. Annoyed; bothered
16. To separate from the group; set apart
17. Characterized by secret movement; avoiding notice
18. Deliberate deception for unfair or unlawful gain
19. In complete agreement
20. Thoughtful

Down
1. Inconspicuous; undistinguished; not well-known
2. Given over to another for care or protection
3. Swayed back and forth unsteadily in a seesaw motion
4. Obtained
5. Unfailing; always correct
6. Settlement of differences in which concessions are made
7. Hindered
8. Something not obvious
9. Fearful feeling; dread
12. Not likely
13. Without sophistication; artless; innocent
14. To keep in existence; maintain; prolong
15. Extreme harshness; rigor

Mockingbird Vocabulary Crossword 3 Answer Key

Across
5. Things that cause trouble, lack of ease, or difficulty
10. Poor person
11. Danger
13. Annoyed; bothered
16. To separate from the group; set apart
17. Characterized by secret movement; avoiding notice
18. Deliberate deception for unfair or unlawful gain
19. In complete agreement
20. Thoughtful

Down
1. Inconspicuous; undistinguished; not well-known
2. Given over to another for care or protection
3. Swayed back and forth unsteadily in a seesaw motion
4. Obtained
5. Unfailing; always correct
6. Settlement of differences in which concessions are made
7. Hindered
8. Something not obvious
9. Fearful feeling; dread
12. Not likely
13. Without sophistication; artless; innocent
14. To keep in existence; maintain; prolong
15. Extreme harshness; rigor

Mockingbird Vocabulary Crossword 4

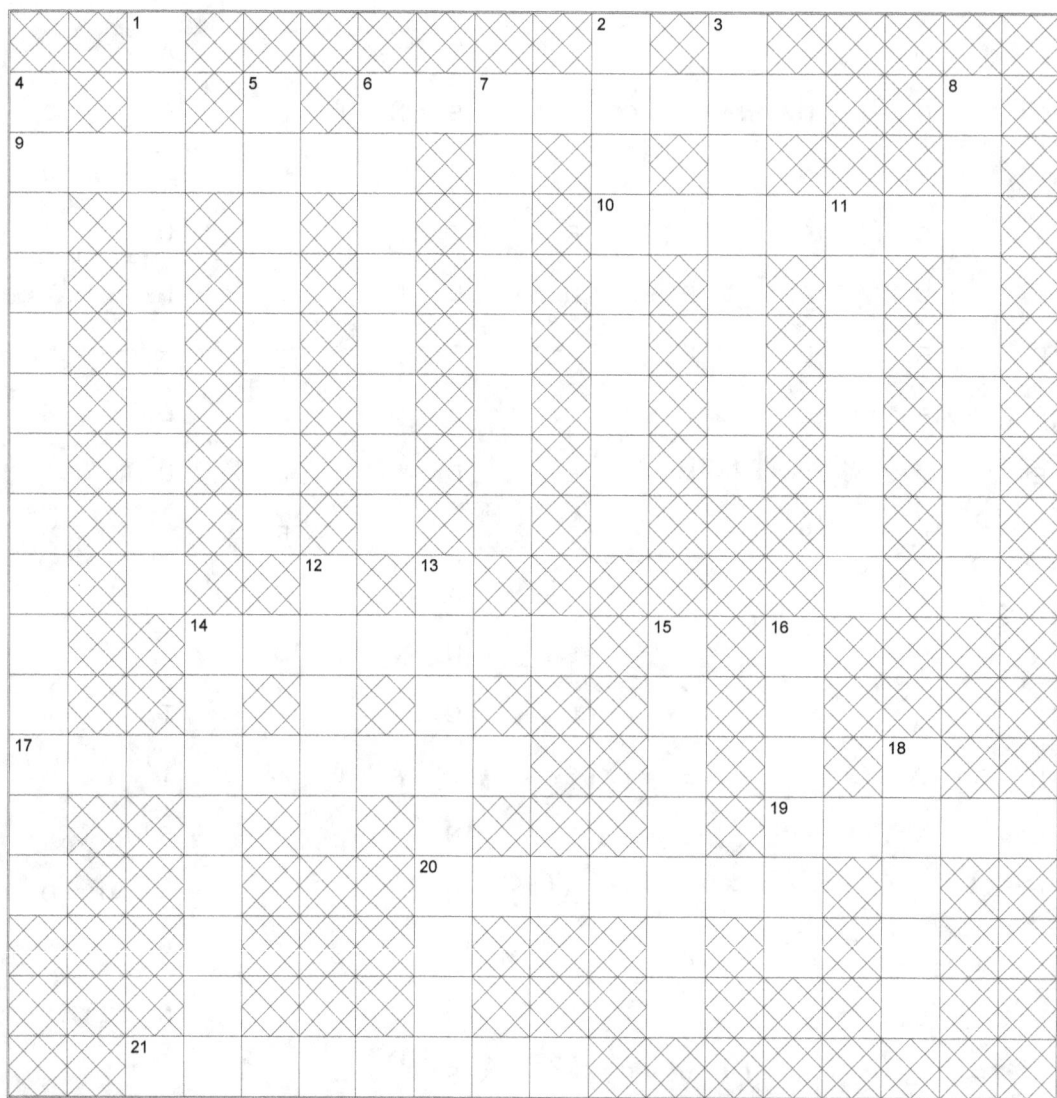

Across
6. Deserted
9. Inconspicuous; undistinguished; not well-known
10. Act of avoiding
14. Extreme harshness; rigor
17. Without sophistication; artless; innocent
19. Danger
20. To separate from the group; set apart
21. Close to; next to

Down
1. Evaluation
2. Supposedly; believed to be so but not yet proved to be so
3. Characterized by secret movement; avoiding notice
4. Of or about the same age
5. Activities; hobbies
6. Deliberating; considering
7. Something not obvious
8. Agreed to
11. To allow one a special pleasure
12. Deliberate deception for unfair or unlawful gain
13. Unable to be heard
14. Swayed back and forth unsteadily in a seesaw motion
15. To forcibly draw forth; pull out
16. Poor person
18. Annoyed; bothered

Mockingbird Vocabulary Crossword 4 Answer Key

Across
6. Deserted
9. Inconspicuous; undistinguished; not well-known
10. Act of avoiding
14. Extreme harshness; rigor
17. Without sophistication; artless; innocent
19. Danger
20. To separate from the group; set apart
21. Close to; next to

Down
1. Evaluation
2. Supposedly; believed to be so but not yet proved to be so
3. Characterized by secret movement; avoiding notice
4. Of or about the same age
5. Activities; hobbies
6. Deliberating; considering
7. Something not obvious
8. Agreed to
11. To allow one a special pleasure
12. Deliberate deception for unfair or unlawful gain
13. Unable to be heard
14. Swayed back and forth unsteadily in a seesaw motion
15. To forcibly draw forth; pull out
16. Poor person
18. Annoyed; bothered

Mockingbird Vocabulary Juggle Letters 1

1. NUMOUNIAS = 1. _____
   In complete agreement

2. SNEIGUONU = 2. _____
   Without sophistication; artless; innocent

3. TEEVAINLRR = 3. _____
   not applicable; having nothing to do with the matter at hand

4. PEICHSTRYO = 4. _____
   People who say they believe one thing but actually believe in the opposite

5. CUNSNIICOPUOS = 5. _____
   Not readily noticeable

6. MPOMOESCRI = 6. _____
   Settlement of differences in which concessions are made

7. EGIMOTNTNR = 7. _____
   Harassing; bothering; pestering

8. RMUTCENNOSPOEN = 8. _____
   Authoritative statements

9. EBDUGERG = 9. _____
   To envy the possession or enjoyment of something

10. ONCDEESTN =10. _____
    Agreed to

11. NETJAADC =11. _____
    Close to; next to

12. TCUEPAOIRPONC =12. _____
    The absorption of the attention or intellect

13. EDDEDNNCSCEO =13. _____
    Bring one's self down to an inferior level

14. MTTIIIDNIAON =14. _____
    Threats

15. STRTEDNEU =15. _____
    Given over to another for care or protection

Mockingbird Vocabulary Juggle Letters 1 Answer Key

1. NUMOUNIAS = 1. UNANIMOUS
   In complete agreement

2. SNEIGUONU = 2. INGENUOUS
   Without sophistication; artless; innocent

3. TEEVAINLRR = 3. IRRELEVANT
   not applicable; having nothing to do with the matter at hand

4. PEICHSTRYO = 4. HYPOCRITES
   People who say they believe one thing but actually believe in the opposite

5. CUNSNIICOPUOS = 5. INCONSPICUOUS
   Not readily noticeable

6. MPOMOESCRI = 6. COMPROMISE
   Settlement of differences in which concessions are made

7. EGIMOTNTNR = 7. TORMENTING
   Harassing; bothering; pestering

8. RMUTCENNOSPOEN = 8. PRONOUNCEMENTS
   Authoritative statements

9. EBDUGERG = 9. BEGRUDGE
   To envy the possession or enjoyment of something

10. ONCDEESTN =10. CONSENTED
    Agreed to

11. NETJAADC =11. ADJACENT
    Close to; next to

12. TCUEPAOIRPONC =12. PREOCCUPATION
    The absorption of the attention or intellect

13. EDDEDNNCSCEO =13. CONDESCENDED
    Bring one's self down to an inferior level

14. MTTIIIDNIAON =14. INTIMIDATION
    Threats

15. STRTEDNEU =15. ENTRUSTED
    Given over to another for care or protection

Mockingbird Vocabulary Juggle Letters 2

1. OCECESDNEDDN = 1. _____
Bring one's self down to an inferior level

2. EENRDTUTS = 2. _____
Given over to another for care or protection

3. EATKROASNUCN = 3. _____
Contrary; disagreeable; quarrelsome

4. ATNGLINAM = 4. _____
Actively evil in nature

5. LSACELIISACCET = 5. _____
Pertaining to church

6. IIEVEMTTAD = 6. _____
Thoughtful; reflective

7. YPPREETLXI = 7. _____
The condition of being puzzled

8. TCACPUOIONREP = 8. _____
The absorption of the attention or intellect

9. NINTIIODMIAT = 9. _____
Threats

10. LILAEIFLNB = 10. _____
Unfailing; always correct

11. AFLNACATI = 11. _____
Possessed or driven by excessive zeal

12. ERMOPTSAICNERO = 12. _____
Of or about the same age

13. UTTYSBEL = 13. _____
Something not obvious

14. UILEBADNI = 14. _____
Unable to be heard

15. UGBNIIQBL = 15. _____
Making petty distinctions or irrelevant observations

Mockingbird Vocabulary Juggle Letters 2 Answer Key

1. OCECESDNEDDN = 1. CONDESCENDED
   Bring one's self down to an inferior level

2. EENRDTUTS = 2. ENTRUSTED
   Given over to another for care or protection

3. EATKROASNUCN = 3. CANTANKEROUS
   Contrary; disagreeable; quarrelsome

4. ATNGLINAM = 4. MALIGNANT
   Actively evil in nature

5. LSACELIISACCET = 5. ECCLESIASTICAL
   Pertaining to church

6. IIEVEMTTAD = 6. MEDITATIVE
   Thoughtful; reflective

7. YPPREETLXI = 7. PERPLEXITY
   The condition of being puzzled

8. TCACPUOIONREP = 8. PREOCCUPATION
   The absorption of the attention or intellect

9. NINTIIODMIAT = 9. INTIMIDATION
   Threats

10. LILAEIFLNB = 10. INFALLIBLE
    Unfailing; always correct

11. AFLNACATI = 11. FANATICAL
    Possessed or driven by excessive zeal

12. ERMOPTSAICNERO = 12. CONTEMPORARIES
    Of or about the same age

13. UTTYSBEL = 13. SUBTLETY
    Something not obvious

14. UILEBADNI = 14. INAUDIBLE
    Unable to be heard

15. UGBNIIQBL = 15. QUIBBLING
    Making petty distinctions or irrelevant observations

Mockingbird Vocabulary Juggle Letters 3

1. PRETCOYIHS = 1. _____
People who say they believe one thing but actually believe in the opposite

2. TNETIGOMNR = 2. _____
Harassing; bothering; pestering

3. ETEETDER = 3. _____
Swayed back and forth unsteadily in a seesaw motion

4. NEDCMUERBE = 4. _____
Hindered

5. UNSGNUEIO = 5. _____
Without sophistication; artless; innocent

6. SIOOEMRATNERPC = 6. _____
Of or about the same age

7. ICREJDPEU = 7. _____
Preconceived preference or idea; bias

8. ANITNGAML = 8. _____
Actively evil in nature

9. APCORPNITEOUC = 9. _____
The absorption of the attention or intellect

10. EANCTJAD = 10. _____
Close to; next to

11. RTECTAX = 11. _____
To forcibly draw forth; pull out

12. LTEEANOMVL = 12. _____
Having ill-will; malicious

13. BMLAYAI = 13. _____
Good-naturedly; cordially

14. GGEBEUDR = 14. _____
To envy the possession or enjoyment of something

15. NGRETASINICA = 15. _____
Finding out

Mockingbird Vocabulary Juggle Letters 3 Answer Key

1. PRETCOYIHS = 1. HYPOCRITES
People who say they believe one thing but actually believe in the opposite

2. TNETIGOMNR = 2. TORMENTING
Harassing; bothering; pestering

3. ETEETDER = 3. TEETERED
Swayed back and forth unsteadily in a seesaw motion

4. NEDCMUERBE = 4. ENCUMBERED
Hindered

5. UNSGNUEIO = 5. INGENUOUS
Without sophistication; artless; innocent

6. SIOOEMRATNERPC = 6. CONTEMPORARIES
Of or about the same age

7. ICREJDPEU = 7. PREJUDICE
Preconceived preference or idea; bias

8. ANITNGAML = 8. MALIGNANT
Actively evil in nature

9. APCORPNITEOUC = 9. PREOCCUPATION
The absorption of the attention or intellect

10. EANCTJAD = 10. ADJACENT
Close to; next to

11. RTECTAX = 11. EXTRACT
To forcibly draw forth; pull out

12. LTEEANOMVL = 12. MALEVOLENT
Having ill-will; malicious

13. BMLAYAI = 13. AMIABLY
Good-naturedly; cordially

14. GGEBEUDR = 14. BEGRUDGE
To envy the possession or enjoyment of something

15. NGRETASINICA = 15. ASCERTAINING
Finding out

Mockingbird Vocabulary Juggle Letters 4

1. ELTMAVNOEL = 1. _____
   Having ill-will; malicious

2. AAFLNICTA = 2. _____
   Possessed or driven by excessive zeal

3. LAETTYSH = 3. _____
   Characterized by secret movement; avoiding notice

4. NTOAEASURKCN = 4. _____
   Contrary; disagreeable; quarrelsome

5. SIUTURPS = 5. _____
   Activities; hobbies

6. RMLOBEAPBI = 6. _____
   Not likely

7. ATGNANILM = 7. _____
   Actively evil in nature

8. EONHEMCLA = 8. _____
   Changeable; like the lizard known for changing colors to blend in with its surroundings

9. OLSVUBIIO = 9. _____
   Unaware

10. IAECUTNADQ =10. _____
    Made familiar with

11. RETUTNEDS =11. _____
    Given over to another for care or protection

12. LIOASET =12. _____
    To separate from the group; set apart

13. GGEDBRUE =13. _____
    To envy the possession or enjoyment of something

14. CRETTAX =14. _____
    To forcibly draw forth; pull out

15. REPUPA =15. _____
    Poor person

Mockingbird Vocabulary Juggle Letters 4 Answer Key

1. ELTMAVNOEL = 1. MALEVOLENT
Having ill-will; malicious

2. AAFLNICTA = 2. FANATICAL
Possessed or driven by excessive zeal

3. LAETTYSH = 3. STEALTHY
Characterized by secret movement; avoiding notice

4. NTOAEASURKCN = 4. CANTANKEROUS
Contrary; disagreeable; quarrelsome

5. SIUTURPS = 5. PURSUITS
Activities; hobbies

6. RMLOBEAPBI = 6. IMPROBABLE
Not likely

7. ATGNANILM = 7. MALIGNANT
Actively evil in nature

8. EONHEMCLA = 8. CHAMELEON
Changeable; like the lizard known for changing colors to blend in with its surroundings

9. OLSVUBIIO = 9. OBLIVIOUS
Unaware

10. IAECUTNADQ = 10. ACQUAINTED
Made familiar with

11. RETUTNEDS = 11. ENTRUSTED
Given over to another for care or protection

12. LIOASET = 12. ISOLATE
To separate from the group; set apart

13. GGEDBRUE = 13. BEGRUDGE
To envy the possession or enjoyment of something

14. CRETTAX = 14. EXTRACT
To forcibly draw forth; pull out

15. REPUPA = 15. PAUPER
Poor person

ACQUAINTED	Made familiar with
ACQUIESCENCE	Passive agreement
ACQUIRED	Obtained
ADJACENT	Close to; next to
ALLEGEDLY	Supposedly; believed to be so but not yet proved to be so
AMIABLY	Good-naturedly; cordially

ANTAGONIZE	Incur the dislike of someone; counteract
APPREHENSION	Fearful feeling; dread
ASCERTAINING	Finding out
ASSESSMENT	Evaluation
BEGRUDGE	To envy the possession or enjoyment of something
CANTANKEROUS	Contrary; disagreeable; quarrelsome

CHAMELEON	Changeable; like the lizard known for changing colors to blend with its surroundings
COMPENSATION	Something given or received as substitution or payment
COMPLACENTLY	In a self-satisfied manner
COMPROMISE	Settlement of differences in which concessions are made
CONDESCENDED	Bring one's self down to an inferior level
CONSENTED	Agreed to

CONTEMPORARIES	Of or about the same age
CONTRADICT	To go against
DEBATING	Deliberating; considering
DEFENDANT	Person against whom an action is brought
DESOLATE	Deserted
DISPELLED	To have done away with

ECCENTRIC	Departing from the established norm, model or rule
ECCLESIASTICAL	Pertaining to church
ENCUMBERED	Hindered
ENTRUSTED	Given over to another for care or protection
EVASION	Act of avoiding
EXTRACT	To forcibly draw forth; pull out

FANATICAL	Possessed or driven by excessive zeal
FRAUD	Deliberate deception for unfair or unlawful gain
HYPOCRITES	People who say they believe one thing but actually believe in the opposite
IMPROBABLE	Not likely
INAUDIBLE	Unable to be heard
INCONSPICUOUS	Not readily noticeable

INCONVENIENCES	Things that cause trouble, lack of ease, or difficulty
INDIGENOUS	Native
INDULGE	To allow one a special pleasure
INEVITABLE	Unavoidable; bound to happen
INFALLIBLE	Unfailing; always correct
INGENUOUS	Without sophistication; artless; innocent

INTIMIDATION	Threats
IRKED	Annoyed; bothered
IRRELEVANT	not applicable; having nothing to do with the matter at hand
ISOLATE	To separate from the group; set apart
MALEVOLENT	Having ill-will; malicious
MALIGNANT	Actively evil in nature

MEDITATIVE	Thoughtful; reflective
OBLIVIOUS	Unaware
OBSCURE	Inconspicuous; undistinguished; not well-known
PAUPER	Poor person
PENSIVE	Thoughtful
PERIL	Danger

PERPLEXITY	The condition of being puzzled
PERSECUTED	Oppressed; ill-treated and harassed
PERSEVERE	Remain constant to a purpose in spite of obstacles
PREDICAMENT	Troublesome situation
PREJUDICE	Preconceived preference or idea; bias
PREOCCUPATION	The absorption of the attention or intellect

PRONOUNCEMENTS	Authoritative statements
PURSUITS	Activities; hobbies
QUIBBLING	Making petty distinctions or irrelevant observations
STEALTHY	Characterized by secret movement; avoiding notice
SUBSEQUENT	Coming after
SUBTLETY	Something not obvious

SUSTAIN	To keep in existence; maintain; prolong
TEETERED	Swayed back and forth unsteadily in a seesaw motion
TORMENTING	Harassing; bothering; pestering
TYRANNY	Extreme harshness; rigor
UNANIMOUS	In complete agreement

Mockingbird Vocabulary

ANTAGONIZE	QUIBBLING	ECCLESIASTICAL	INCONVENIENCES	PURSUITS
PREDICAMENT	FRAUD	DISPELLED	ACQUAINTED	HYPOCRITES
DEBATING	SUBTLETY	FREE SPACE	CONTRADICT	OBSCURE
INAUDIBLE	EXTRACT	TORMENTING	BEGRUDGE	INEVITABLE
PERPLEXITY	PERSEVERE	ASSESSMENT	PAUPER	INCONSPICUOUS

Mockingbird Vocabulary

INFALLIBLE	ACQUIRED	INDIGENOUS	PENSIVE	PREJUDICE
IRRELEVANT	FANATICAL	UNANIMOUS	MEDITATIVE	CANTANKEROUS
SUSTAIN	ALLEGEDLY	FREE SPACE	TYRANNY	ENCUMBERED
DEFENDANT	MALEVOLENT	ECCENTRIC	PRONOUNCEMENTS	AMIABLY
APPREHENSION	STEALTHY	ENTRUSTED	ASCERTAINING	DESOLATE

Mockingbird Vocabulary

INCONVENIENCES	PRONOUNCEMENTS	EXTRACT	SUSTAIN	ADJACENT
CHAMELEON	ISOLATE	PENSIVE	QUIBBLING	CANTANKEROUS
ENTRUSTED	PERSECUTED	FREE SPACE	INDULGE	DISPELLED
SUBSEQUENT	DEFENDANT	ENCUMBERED	DESOLATE	MEDITATIVE
PREJUDICE	COMPLACENTLY	IMPROBABLE	ANTAGONIZE	APPREHENSION

Mockingbird Vocabulary

UNANIMOUS	PERIL	FRAUD	PERSEVERE	ACQUIESCENCE
PREOCCUPATION	ACQUIRED	ECCLESIASTICAL	ECCENTRIC	IRRELEVANT
TEETERED	DEBATING	FREE SPACE	INDIGENOUS	OBSCURE
OBLIVIOUS	ASCERTAINING	COMPROMISE	PURSUITS	PAUPER
IRKED	COMPENSATION	INFALLIBLE	FANATICAL	ACQUAINTED

Mockingbird Vocabulary

INDULGE	INGENUOUS	UNANIMOUS	PREJUDICE	INCONVENIENCES
PERIL	TORMENTING	ALLEGEDLY	MALIGNANT	IMPROBABLE
INEVITABLE	COMPENSATION	FREE SPACE	PENSIVE	SUBTLETY
INAUDIBLE	ECCENTRIC	INDIGENOUS	ISOLATE	PREDICAMENT
EXTRACT	FRAUD	ACQUIESCENCE	CONTEMPORARIES	INCONSPICUOUS

Mockingbird Vocabulary

BEGRUDGE	INFALLIBLE	PAUPER	HYPOCRITES	PRONOUNCEMENTS
ANTAGONIZE	PERSEVERE	AMIABLY	COMPLACENTLY	MEDITATIVE
CONTRADICT	APPREHENSION	FREE SPACE	ASCERTAINING	ASSESSMENT
TYRANNY	SUSTAIN	PERPLEXITY	INTIMIDATION	IRKED
ACQUIRED	ACQUAINTED	SUBSEQUENT	DESOLATE	PERSECUTED

Mockingbird Vocabulary

IMPROBABLE	INCONSPICUOUS	ECCLESIASTICAL	MEDITATIVE	PENSIVE
OBSCURE	CHAMELEON	ACQUIRED	INFALLIBLE	ACQUIESCENCE
OBLIVIOUS	SUBSEQUENT	FREE SPACE	CONTEMPORARIES	DEBATING
PAUPER	CONSENTED	APPREHENSION	SUSTAIN	INDULGE
INTIMIDATION	PURSUITS	PREJUDICE	ECCENTRIC	MALEVOLENT

Mockingbird Vocabulary

BEGRUDGE	FANATICAL	STEALTHY	ISOLATE	INDIGENOUS
CANTANKEROUS	TORMENTING	FRAUD	COMPLACENTLY	ASCERTAINING
ASSESSMENT	EXTRACT	FREE SPACE	QUIBBLING	CONTRADICT
DESOLATE	INEVITABLE	IRRELEVANT	CONDESCENDED	DISPELLED
SUBTLETY	TYRANNY	PERSEVERE	INAUDIBLE	AMIABLY

Mockingbird Vocabulary

CONTEMPORARIES	ADJACENT	INTIMIDATION	DEFENDANT	EXTRACT
ASSESSMENT	MALIGNANT	TEETERED	ACQUIRED	CONSENTED
INCONSPICUOUS	CANTANKEROUS	FREE SPACE	PURSUITS	CONTRADICT
INCONVENIENCES	PAUPER	INDULGE	ENCUMBERED	UNANIMOUS
INDIGENOUS	SUBSEQUENT	MALEVOLENT	INFALLIBLE	ISOLATE

Mockingbird Vocabulary

OBLIVIOUS	TORMENTING	PERSECUTED	QUIBBLING	ALLEGEDLY
TYRANNY	ENTRUSTED	ACQUAINTED	PREOCCUPATION	IMPROBABLE
ACQUIESCENCE	SUBTLETY	FREE SPACE	COMPENSATION	INEVITABLE
CONDESCENDED	BEGRUDGE	COMPLACENTLY	CHAMELEON	ECCLESIASTICAL
PREDICAMENT	COMPROMISE	MEDITATIVE	EVASION	APPREHENSION

Mockingbird Vocabulary

ASSESSMENT	INAUDIBLE	EVASION	ASCERTAINING	ANTAGONIZE
TYRANNY	DISPELLED	FANATICAL	INDIGENOUS	CONDESCENDED
ENCUMBERED	APPREHENSION	FREE SPACE	DEFENDANT	IMPROBABLE
AMIABLY	OBSCURE	SUSTAIN	INCONSPICUOUS	MEDITATIVE
PENSIVE	IRRELEVANT	ACQUIESCENCE	PERSEVERE	INDULGE

Mockingbird Vocabulary

CONTRADICT	IRKED	TORMENTING	INGENUOUS	INTIMIDATION
PURSUITS	DEBATING	ECCENTRIC	PAUPER	PREJUDICE
COMPROMISE	COMPLACENTLY	FREE SPACE	PERPLEXITY	PERIL
CANTANKEROUS	ACQUAINTED	STEALTHY	BEGRUDGE	TEETERED
OBLIVIOUS	UNANIMOUS	ADJACENT	INEVITABLE	CONSENTED

Mockingbird Vocabulary

FANATICAL	PERSEVERE	DISPELLED	ACQUAINTED	BEGRUDGE
PREJUDICE	IMPROBABLE	INGENUOUS	INTIMIDATION	INAUDIBLE
MALIGNANT	EVASION	FREE SPACE	COMPLACENTLY	TEETERED
CANTANKEROUS	ECCLESIASTICAL	ACQUIRED	APPREHENSION	COMPROMISE
MEDITATIVE	DEFENDANT	PRONOUNCEMENTS	INEVITABLE	ACQUIESCENCE

Mockingbird Vocabulary

UNANIMOUS	HYPOCRITES	ALLEGEDLY	MALEVOLENT	PAUPER
CHAMELEON	INDULGE	CONTRADICT	AMIABLY	ENTRUSTED
TYRANNY	INCONVENIENCES	FREE SPACE	SUSTAIN	INFALLIBLE
CONSENTED	TORMENTING	ECCENTRIC	ANTAGONIZE	ASCERTAINING
CONTEMPORARIES	INDIGENOUS	PREDICAMENT	OBLIVIOUS	OBSCURE

Mockingbird Vocabulary

PRONOUN CEMENTS	PERSEVERE	ACQUIRED	ALLEGEDLY	ECCLESIASTICAL
APPREHENSION	INCONSPICUOUS	SUBSEQUENT	ACQUAINTED	INFALLIBLE
TYRANNY	COMPROMISE	FREE SPACE	IRRELEVANT	CONDESCENDED
FRAUD	IRKED	PURSUITS	PAUPER	TEETERED
PERSECUTED	CONTEMPORARIES	EXTRACT	ANTAGONIZE	PREOCCUPATION

Mockingbird Vocabulary

CANTANKEROUS	PENSIVE	ASCERTAINING	INEVITABLE	INAUDIBLE
PERPLEXITY	INDULGE	OBLIVIOUS	MEDITATIVE	FANATICAL
DEFENDANT	COMPLACENTLY	FREE SPACE	CONTRADICT	CONSENTED
INCONVENIENCES	ENTRUSTED	DESOLATE	TORMENTING	ACQUIESCENCE
SUBTLETY	ASSESSMENT	EVASION	DISPELLED	ADJACENT

Mockingbird Vocabulary

PAUPER	DEBATING	COMPROMISE	PREOCCUPATION	INCONSPICUOUS
SUBTLETY	INGENUOUS	FRAUD	ECCENTRIC	IRRELEVANT
PRONOUNCEMENTS	INDULGE	FREE SPACE	ASSESSMENT	MEDITATIVE
APPREHENSION	EXTRACT	TEETERED	ENTRUSTED	INAUDIBLE
INFALLIBLE	OBSCURE	CONSENTED	ACQUAINTED	ADJACENT

Mockingbird Vocabulary

PERSECUTED	EVASION	UNANIMOUS	CONTEMPORARIES	CHAMELEON
INDIGENOUS	MALEVOLENT	CANTANKEROUS	ECCLESIASTICAL	DESOLATE
PREDICAMENT	FANATICAL	FREE SPACE	QUIBBLING	PERIL
ACQUIRED	INCONVENIENCES	SUBSEQUENT	IRKED	PERSEVERE
ASCERTAINING	ENCUMBERED	STEALTHY	PREJUDICE	BEGRUDGE

Mockingbird Vocabulary

INCONSPICUOUS	INFALLIBLE	ANTAGONIZE	PURSUITS	COMPENSATION
CONDESCENDED	ALLEGEDLY	PENSIVE	INEVITABLE	EVASION
INAUDIBLE	IRKED	FREE SPACE	ENTRUSTED	SUBTLETY
INDULGE	DEFENDANT	BEGRUDGE	CHAMELEON	DISPELLED
INCONVENIENCES	CONSENTED	MEDITATIVE	FANATICAL	MALIGNANT

Mockingbird Vocabulary

TYRANNY	PERSECUTED	PERIL	UNANIMOUS	AMIABLY
STEALTHY	EXTRACT	ACQUIRED	MALEVOLENT	ECCLESIASTICAL
OBSCURE	PREDICAMENT	FREE SPACE	ASSESSMENT	INGENUOUS
SUSTAIN	ACQUAINTED	FRAUD	ACQUIESCENCE	IMPROBABLE
CANTANKEROUS	SUBSEQUENT	OBLIVIOUS	IRRELEVANT	ENCUMBERED

Mockingbird Vocabulary

TYRANNY	ADJACENT	MALIGNANT	CANTANKEROUS	PURSUITS
UNANIMOUS	PREOCCUPATION	CONDESCENDED	INTIMIDATION	PERIL
IRRELEVANT	ASCERTAINING	FREE SPACE	PRONOUNCEMENTS	INGENUOUS
BEGRUDGE	INEVITABLE	CHAMELEON	FANATICAL	PREDICAMENT
IMPROBABLE	INFALLIBLE	AMIABLY	ACQUIRED	COMPENSATION

Mockingbird Vocabulary

ACQUIESCENCE	INCONSPICUOUS	CONTEMPORARIES	MALEVOLENT	DEFENDANT
ASSESSMENT	HYPOCRITES	TEETERED	INAUDIBLE	ENTRUSTED
PERSECUTED	INDULGE	FREE SPACE	SUSTAIN	PERSEVERE
QUIBBLING	DISPELLED	DEBATING	ANTAGONIZE	EXTRACT
SUBSEQUENT	COMPROMISE	EVASION	FRAUD	ENCUMBERED

Mockingbird Vocabulary

ADJACENT	BEGRUDGE	MEDITATIVE	INCONSPICUOUS	ENTRUSTED
ECCLESIASTICAL	ACQUIRED	HYPOCRITES	FANATICAL	INGENUOUS
EXTRACT	IRKED	FREE SPACE	EVASION	PREDICAMENT
OBSCURE	ISOLATE	INTIMIDATION	ANTAGONIZE	QUIBBLING
CONTRADICT	CHAMELEON	IMPROBABLE	PREOCCUPATION	ACQUIESCENCE

Mockingbird Vocabulary

DESOLATE	INEVITABLE	FRAUD	MALIGNANT	PERPLEXITY
PURSUITS	CANTANKEROUS	COMPLACENTLY	ENCUMBERED	INFALLIBLE
CONTEMPORARIES	IRRELEVANT	FREE SPACE	INDIGENOUS	TEETERED
MALEVOLENT	PERSEVERE	PERIL	COMPROMISE	SUBSEQUENT
AMIABLY	ALLEGEDLY	PENSIVE	TORMENTING	INCONVENIENCES

Mockingbird Vocabulary

ALLEGEDLY	CHAMELEON	FANATICAL	ASSESSMENT	PERSEVERE
QUIBBLING	UNANIMOUS	ENTRUSTED	MALEVOLENT	INCONVENIENCES
OBLIVIOUS	DISPELLED	FREE SPACE	INDULGE	ISOLATE
PERPLEXITY	SUBTLETY	OBSCURE	SUBSEQUENT	CONSENTED
HYPOCRITES	STEALTHY	ACQUAINTED	COMPENSATION	CANTANKEROUS

Mockingbird Vocabulary

ASCERTAINING	TORMENTING	TEETERED	ENCUMBERED	BEGRUDGE
PURSUITS	IRRELEVANT	ACQUIRED	PERSECUTED	PREDICAMENT
IMPROBABLE	PENSIVE	FREE SPACE	PAUPER	CONTRADICT
INDIGENOUS	INFALLIBLE	ECCENTRIC	INCONSPICUOUS	PERIL
ACQUIESCENCE	CONTEMPORARIES	PREJUDICE	AMIABLY	FRAUD

Mockingbird Vocabulary

DESOLATE	ASCERTAINING	ECCLESIASTICAL	PAUPER	STEALTHY
CONTRADICT	TYRANNY	ADJACENT	ALLEGEDLY	CONDESCENDED
COMPENSATION	PRONOUNCEMENTS	FREE SPACE	DEBATING	INDIGENOUS
CONTEMPORARIES	ENTRUSTED	INFALLIBLE	PERSECUTED	OBSCURE
AMIABLY	IRKED	PENSIVE	APPREHENSION	ECCENTRIC

Mockingbird Vocabulary

BEGRUDGE	CONSENTED	ASSESSMENT	PREJUDICE	CANTANKEROUS
INEVITABLE	DISPELLED	IRRELEVANT	PERPLEXITY	ACQUAINTED
INCONVENIENCES	ISOLATE	FREE SPACE	ACQUIESCENCE	SUBSEQUENT
MALIGNANT	INTIMIDATION	ENCUMBERED	OBLIVIOUS	PREDICAMENT
MALEVOLENT	TORMENTING	ANTAGONIZE	DEFENDANT	QUIBBLING

Mockingbird Vocabulary

CONSENTED	INCONVENIENCES	BEGRUDGE	ACQUIESCENCE	DISPELLED
CONTRADICT	FANATICAL	PREJUDICE	FRAUD	TYRANNY
IMPROBABLE	EXTRACT	FREE SPACE	PRONOUNCEMENTS	HYPOCRITES
ADJACENT	PERSEVERE	QUIBBLING	PERPLEXITY	OBSCURE
ENCUMBERED	INGENUOUS	COMPLACENTLY	CHAMELEON	PREOCCUPATION

Mockingbird Vocabulary

PAUPER	OBLIVIOUS	IRRELEVANT	DEBATING	EVASION
ASSESSMENT	PERSECUTED	ENTRUSTED	APPREHENSION	TEETERED
INDIGENOUS	CANTANKEROUS	FREE SPACE	ANTAGONIZE	PREDICAMENT
SUSTAIN	CONTEMPORARIES	ECCLESIASTICAL	ASCERTAINING	SUBTLETY
INTIMIDATION	TORMENTING	ACQUIRED	SUBSEQUENT	IRKED

Mockingbird Vocabulary

ECCLESIASTICAL	FANATICAL	IRKED	FRAUD	PERIL
INTIMIDATION	DEFENDANT	CONTEMPORARIES	ACQUIRED	ALLEGEDLY
CHAMELEON	PURSUITS	FREE SPACE	TORMENTING	ACQUAINTED
INFALLIBLE	EXTRACT	PAUPER	PRONOUNCEMENTS	IMPROBABLE
CANTANKEROUS	MEDITATIVE	PREOCCUPATION	PENSIVE	APPREHENSION

Mockingbird Vocabulary

ASSESSMENT	STEALTHY	INEVITABLE	TYRANNY	INAUDIBLE
ISOLATE	ANTAGONIZE	MALIGNANT	ASCERTAINING	SUBSEQUENT
TEETERED	CONSENTED	FREE SPACE	PERPLEXITY	COMPLACENTLY
MALEVOLENT	SUBTLETY	PREDICAMENT	ENTRUSTED	CONTRADICT
EVASION	OBLIVIOUS	ACQUIESCENCE	INCONSPICUOUS	DESOLATE

www.ingramcontent.com/pod-product-compliance
Lightning Source LLC
Chambersburg PA
CBHW081454070526
44586CB00019B/2344